Lifts in Berlin

Fahrstühle in Berlin

JOVIS

Lifts in Berlin

100 years of history

With texts by
Kerstin Englert
and
photographs by
Alfred Englert

Fahrstühle in Berlin

Eine 100jährige Geschichte

Mit Texten von
Kerstin Englert
und
Fotografien von
Alfred Englert

JOVIS

Inhalt Contents

Foreword

This illustrated book makes it impressively clear how attractive something purely functional can be – such as vertical transport that is as comfortable and fast as possible. The invention of the lift not only had a lasting effect on architecture and paved the way for the construction of tall buildings. The lifts themselves are remarkable examples of architecture in their own right.

Lifts have often been acclaimed as documents of technical history. To consider them from an architectural point of view is a new venture. This book, in which the text and the illustrations supplement and reinforce each other in an outstanding way, offers insights into the history of styles in the late 19th and the 20th century. It covers the development from Historicism and Art Nouveau through New Functionalism to the transparency of modern lift architecture.

The objects that are so exquisitely illustrated here have in fact been one of the greatest and most reliable pillars of the economy of Berlin since the end of the 19th century. Lift production even had its place while Berlin was a divided city. And this is of course all the more true now in the course of reunification.

In the wonderful photographs of early lifts, one thing seems to me to be particularly clear: the fact that greatest demand for this means of transport arose within the city of Berlin was not only an advantage for production, it also brought benefits for lifts as a cultural phenomenon. The work was needed directly outside the factory gates. That is still just as true today.

Lifts therefore provide information in several respects. They give an insight into the architectural expansion of a metropolitan city like Berlin, they are an important testimony to technical progress and their design reflects the development of architecture.

This illustrated book has given a face to the architecture of lifts. And I must say that it is an attractive face!

Volker Hassemer

Vorwort

Dieser Bildband macht in eindrucksvoller Weise klar, wie attraktiv so etwas zunächst rein Funktionales wie eine möglichst bequeme und schnelle Beförderung der vertikalen Art sein kann. Die Erfindung des Lifts, dies ist zu sehen, hat nicht nur nachhaltig die Baukunst beeinflußt, indem sie der Entwicklung der Hochhaus-Architektur den Weg bereitete. Die Lifte selbst sind bemerkenswerte Beispiele von Baukunst.

Als Dokumente der Technikgeschichte wurden Aufzüge bereits des öfteren gewürdigt. Neu ist aber ihre Betrachtung aus architektonischer Sicht. Die vorliegende Publikation, in dem sich Wort und Bild in hervorragender Weise ergänzen und stärken, bietet Einblick in die Stilgeschichte des ausgehenden Jahrhunderts. Dabei spannt sich der Bogen von Historismus und Jugendstil über Neue Sachlichkeit bis zur Transparenz der heutigen Aufzugsarchitektur.

Was so prachtvoll aussieht, ist einer der bedeutenden und zuverlässigen Pfeiler der Berliner Wirtschaft seit Ende des 19. Jahrhunderts. Die Aufzugsproduktion hat auch in der Zeit des geteilten Berlin immer ihren Platz gehabt. Und jetzt, im Zuge der Wiedervereinigung um so mehr.

Mir scheint es aus den wunderbaren Fotografien gerade der frühen Aufzüge zu sprechen: Hier hat nicht nur die Produktion, sondern auch die Kultur dieses Beförderungsmittels davon profitiert, daß diese Stadt selbst ihr größter Nachfrager war. Die Arbeit wurde direkt vor den Fabriktoren gebraucht. Und dies ist heute noch so.

Aufzüge geben also in mehrfacher Hinsicht Auskunft. Sie bieten einen Einblick in die städtebauliche Erweiterung einer Metropole wie Berlin, sind wichtige Zeugnisse des technischen Fortschritts und spiegeln in ihrer Gestaltung die Entwicklung der Baukunst wider.

Mit diesem Bildband wurde der Aufzugsarchitektur ein Gesicht gegeben, und da kann man nur sagen: sie sieht gut aus!

Volker Hassemer

From Hemp Ropes to Friction Wheel

History and drive mechanisms of passenger lifts

Lifts are found in a variety of places, and many people simply take them for granted. They are happily used, but only rarely appreciated in their architectural design. With a selection of about 110 examples from the last 100 years, this illustrated history of Berlin's lift architecture documents the stylistic development in the design of portals, doors, lift cabins and shaft frames. It ranges from the wealth of forms of late Historicism and Art Nouveau to the reduced design language and transparency of modern lifts. The treatment concentrates on lifts which are still preserved today, or have been restored in their original design, and are in operation.[1]

The invention of the lift points us to the USA and is closely linked with the development of skyscraper architecture which began in the American cities of New York and Chicago. The first multi-storey buildings containing lifts were built in New York in the late 1860s and in Chicago after the fire of 1871. In Germany, however, the prevailing building laws did not permit the construction of tall buildings until 1920. In official documents, the term *Hochhaus* (tall building) was first used in a circular order of 3rd January 1921 by the Prussian Minister of Welfare, and it was supplemented on 29th September 1921 by a definition that a *Hochhaus* was deemed to be a new building which contained more than six full storeys and served commercial purposes – with the exception of factories, warehouses and similar buildings.[2]

The first lifts in Berlin were not in these new tall buildings, but in rented apartment buildings with three to five storeys. The architects who planned rented apartment buildings in Berlin at the beginning of the 20th century included Albert Gessner. He dated the origination of the

Vom Hanfseil zum Haftrad

Geschichte und Antrieb des Personenaufzugs

Aufzüge sind vielerorts anzutreffen und für zahlreiche Menschen selbstverständlich. Obgleich gern genutzt, werden sie jedoch nur selten in ihrer architektonischen Gestaltung gewürdigt. Mit einer Auswahl von rund 110 Beispielen der letzten 100 Jahre dokumentiert diese illustrierte Geschichte der Berliner Aufzugsarchitektur deren stilistische Entwicklung in der Gestaltung der Portale, Türen, Kabinen und Schachtgerüste. Sie reicht von der Formenfülle des Späthistorismus und Jugendstils bis zur reduzierten Gestaltungssprache und Transparenz heutiger Aufzüge. Der Blick konzentriert sich dabei auf jene Anlagen, die heute noch erhalten bzw. in ihrer ursprünglichen Gestaltung wiederhergestellt und in Betrieb sind.[1]

Die Erfindung des Aufzuges weist zunächst in die USA und ist eng mit der Entwicklung der Hochhausarchitektur verbunden, die ihren Anfang in den amerikanischen Großstädten New York und Chicago nahm. Die ersten mehrstöckigen Gebäude mit Aufzügen entstanden in der zweiten Hälfte der 1860er Jahre in New York und ab 1871, nach dem großen Brand, in Chicago. In Deutschland hingegen war nach den bestehenden Baugesetzen die Ausführung hoher Häuser bis 1920 nicht zulässig. Amtlich wird der Begriff »Hochhaus« hier erstmals in einem Runderlaß vom 3. Januar 1921 von dem preußischen Minister für Volkswohlfahrt verwendet und am 29. September 1921 dahingehend ergänzt, daß solche Neubauten als Hochhäuser anzusehen sind, die mehr als sechs Vollgeschosse enhalten und geschäftlichen Zwecken dienen – ausgenommen Fabriken, Speicher und ähnliche Gebäude.[2]

In Berlin begegnen uns die ersten Aufzüge nicht in Hochhäusern, sondern in Mietshäusern mit drei bis fünf Geschossen. Zu jenen Architekten, nach deren Plänen zu Beginn des 20. Jahrhunderts in Berlin Mietshäuser entstanden sind, gehört auch Albert Gessner. Er datiert die Entstehung des Begriffes »Miethaus« etwa in die Zeit des Aufschwungs der 1860er Jahre und versteht diese Gattung in erster Linie als Geschäftsobjekt: »Die Großstadt erfordert naturgemäß eine Konzentration des Wohnungswesens. Diese Konzentration bedingt eine Steigerung ihres Bodenwertes und diese wieder eine Ausnutzung durch das Bauen in Stockwerken. Das Bauen von Stockwerken führte zur Vereinigung mehrerer Wohnungen in einem Hause und damit zum Miethaus.«[3] Bei Gessner wurden Aufzüge frühzeitig in der Gesamtkonzeption berücksichtigt (Abb. 15) und führten ihn bereits 1909 zu der kritischen Frage, ob die repräsentative Treppenanlage »nicht einmal ganz verschwindet, weil die Aufzüge immer vollkommener werden.«[4]

Der Betrachtung der Berliner Aufzugsarchitektur der letzten 100 Jahre wird im folgenden ein Überblick der Geschichte des vertikalen Personentransportes und der unterschiedlichen Antriebsarten sowie eine kurze Erläuterung der Begriffe »Aufzug«, »Fahrstuhl« und »Lift« vorangestellt.

Eines der frühesten Zeugnisse für den vertikalen Personentransport befand sich möglicherweise im Theater von Priene bei Milet, das in frühhellenistischer Zeit zwischen Ende des 4. und Mitte des 3. Jh. v. Chr. errichtet wurde. 1921 stieß der deutsche Archäologe Armin von Gerkan bei Ausgrabungen im Bühnengebäude auf einen Schacht, dessen »eigentliche Bedeutung nur im Obergeschoß gelegen haben [kann], da er im Untergeschoß gar nicht zugänglich war. [...] Für die beschriebene Anlage gibt es nur die eine einwandfreie Erklärung, daß sie eine Aufzugsvorrichtung enthalten haben muß, mit deren Hilfe Göttererscheinungen in der Höhe bewerkstelligt werden konnten. Der Schauspieler trat vom Treppenpodest auf eine Plattform, die

term *Mietshaus* (rented apartment building) back to the boom period in the 1860s, and he regarded this type of building mainly as a commercial object: "A metropolitan city naturally requires a concentration of residential accommodation. This concentration led to an increase in land value, and this in turn led to the utilisation of land by building several storeys. And building several storeys led to the concentration of several dwellings in one building, and thus to the rented apartment building."[3] Gessner included lifts in his overall concept early on (Fig. 15), and this led him in 1909 to pose the critical question of whether magnificent staircases would "eventually disappear completely because lifts are becoming more and more perfect."[4]

Before we come to look at lift architecture in Berlin over the last 100 years, we will first of all consider the general history of vertical passenger transport, different drive mechanisms and the terminology involved.

One of the earliest forms of vertical transport of persons was possibly in the theatre of Priene near Miletus, which was built in the early Hellenistic period between the end of the 4th and the middle of the 3rd century BC. In 1921, during excavations in the stage building, the German archaeologist Armin von Gerkan found a shaft for which "the real significance can only have been at the upper level, because it was not accessible from the lower level. [...] For the installation described there is only one reasonable explanation, i.e. that it must have contained a lift with which appearances of the gods could be staged. The actor stepped from the staircase onto a platform which was hoisted upwards by ropes while at the same time a counterweight moved downwards. The original installation was a completely free design. In the upper position it remained about 50 cm below the edge of the roof because it was sufficient if the actor was seen as far as his knees."[5] According to Gerkan, the size and depth of the shaft exclude the possibility that it could have contained the mast of a rotary crane rather than a lift platform.[6]

Lifts were also known in ancient Rome. In the Forum Romanum, there are said to have been twelve lifting installations for the vertical transport of the gladiators. "The technique was simple," wrote Jeannot Simmen and Uwe Drepper. "Slaves turned wooden winch pulleys; the lift cages did not have any counterweights."[7]

In the lower storey of the Colosseum, three lift systems can at present be distinguished.[8] The first system, which served to transport animals of prey, was at the edge of the arena in the immediate vicinity of the podium. It consisted of cages with a height of about one metre which ran in sliding rails and were pulled by winches under the wooden covering of the arena. The animals could reach the arena via a short ramp. On the basis of the building structure, 32–36 cages have been reconstructed, each with its own winch, in the so-called corridor B. In a second phase, which has not yet been dated, a second system was constructed in the centre of the arena for the transport of persons, although the technical mechanism used is still largely unknown.[9] And there is uncertainty about the existence of a lift in the Domus Aurea, the palace of Emperor Nero built after 64 AD. There are said to be detailed descriptions of this lift, but the excavations even today do not permit any precise reconstruction.[10]

Mediaeval illustrations mainly show hoisting tools for water and loads which were driven by winches and pedal wheels.[11] One of the few examples of vertical passenger transport in the Middle Ages are the illustrative portrayals of the escape of St. Paul from Damascus (Acts 9:25 and 2. Cor. 11:33), for example in the mosaics of the Capella Palatina in Palermo and the cathedral of Monreale dating from the 12th century, and in the author's portrait of Kristan von Hamle in the Manessian song manuscript from the first half of the 14th century. Paul is let down in a basket on a rope which is operated by muscle power by two men. The miniature in the *Manessian song manuscript* (see next page) shows a lady on a castle tower pulling up the courtly love singer, who is sitting in a wooden tub, by means of a

von Stricken nach oben gehoben wurde, während entsprechend ein Gegengewicht in die Tiefe glitt. Bei der ursprünglichen Anlage lag eine völlige Konstruktionsfreiheit vor; sie blieb in der oberen Lage aus Sicherheitsgründen etwa 0,5 m unter dem Dachrande, da es genügte, wenn die Gestalt des Schauspielers bis zum Knie gesehen wurde.«[5] Größe und Tiefe des Schachtes schließen nach Gerkan die Vermutung aus, daß sich darin anstelle einer Hebebühne der Mast eines Drehkranes befunden habe.[6]

Auch im antiken Rom waren Aufzüge bekannt. Im Forum Romanum sollen zwölf Aufzugsanlagen den Vertikaltransport der Gladiatoren ermöglicht haben. »Die Technik war einfach« – so Jeannot Simmen und Uwe Drepper – »Sklaven trieben hölzerne Haspelwinden an; die Aufzugskäfige hatten keine Gegengewichte.«[7]

Im Untergeschoß des Kolosseums sind bisher drei Aufzugsysteme zu unterscheiden.[8] Das erste System, das dem Transport der Raubtiere diente, befand sich am Rande der Arena in unmittelbarer Nähe des Podiums. Es handelte sich dabei um etwa ein Meter hohe Käfige, die in Gleitschienen liefen und mittels Winden bis unter die hölzerne Abdeckung der Arena gezogen wurden. Von dort gelangten die Tiere über eine kurze Rampe auf die Kampfbahn. Aufgrund der baulichen Situation können 32–36 Käfige mit jeweils einer Winde im sogenannten Korridor B rekonstruiert werden. In einer zweiten, bislang nicht datierten Phase errichtete man im Zentrum der Arena ein weiteres System für den Transport von Menschen, dessen Technik allerdings noch weitgehend unbekannt ist.[9] Ungewiß ist auch die Existenz eines Aufzuges in der *Domus Aurea*, dem nach 64 n. Chr. errichteten Palast des Kaisers Nero. Zu diesem Aufzug sollen detaillierte Beschreibungen existieren, obgleich die Grabungsbefunde noch heute keine genaue Rekonstruktion zulassen.[10]

Mittelalterliche Darstellungen zeigen hauptsächlich Hebewerkzeuge für Wasser und Lasten, die durch Haspelwellen und Treträder angetrieben wurden.[11] Zu den wenigen Beispielen des vertikalen Personentransportes im Mittelalter gehören die bildlichen Darstellungen der Flucht des Paulus aus Damaskus (Apg. 9,25 und 2 Kor. 11,33), wie in den Mosaiken der Cappella Palatina in Palermo und im Dom von Monreale aus dem 12. Jahrhundert, sowie das Autorenporträt des Kristan von Hamle in der *Manessischen Liederhandschrift* aus der ersten Hälfte des 14. Jahrhunderts. Paulus wird in einem Korb heruntergelassen, dessen Seil mit reiner Muskelkraft von zwei Männern gehalten wird. Die Miniatur in der *Manessischen Liederhandschrift* zeigt eine Dame auf einem Burgturm, die den in einer Holzbütte sitzenden Minnesänger mit Hilfe einer Seilwinde per Hand heraufzieht.[12] Auch in den Meteora-Klöstern, im griechischen Thessalien auf hohen Felsenplateaus gelegen, wurden die Menschen ursprünglich auf diese Weise in Körben oder Netzen auf- und abwärts transportiert.[13]

Eine der frühesten technischen Anleitungen zum Bau des sogenannten »Fliegenden Stuhles«, dem Vorläufer des Fahrstuhles, datiert aus dem 17. Jahrhundert. Sie stammt von dem Jenaer Wissenschaftler Erhard Weigel (1625–1699) und wurde 1669 in den *Mathematischen Kunstübungen* abgedruckt: »Lanx Reciproca, Eine Fahr-Wage/verborgen in alle Stockwercke des Hauses/ohne Steigen/bequemlich zu kommen/in einem nur drey Schuh breiten Canalangeordnet/welch /vermittelst einer Gegen-Last/einen Menschen/so sich nur ein wenig an denen dar zu geordneten Handhaben anhält/in die Höhe und wieder herunter läßt/da er doch/wo er will/nach belieben/still stehen kan.«[14] Den Prototyp dieser Erfindung hatte Weigel 1670 im eigenen Haus, der *Domus Weigeliana*, installiert, das zu

Autorenporträt des Kristan von Hamle aus der *Manessischen Liederhandschrift,* wohl Zürich nach 1300

Author's portrait of Kristan von Hamle from the *Manessian song manuscript*, probably Zurich, after 1300

rope pulley.[12] In the Meteora monasteries, set on high rock plateaux in the Greek area of Thessaly, people were also originally transported vertically in baskets by this method.[13]

One of the earliest technical guidelines for the construction of the so-called "Flying Chair", the precursor of the lift, dates from the 17th century. It originates from the scientist Erhard Weigel (1625–1699) from Jena, and it was printed in 1669 in the *Mathematische Kunstübungen* (Mathematical exercises): "Lanx Reciproca, a travelling carriage / to travel in comfort / concealed into all storeys of the house / without climbing / in a channel only three shoes wide / which / by means of a counterweight / enables a person / if he can follow the instructions / to let himself up and then down again / because he can / stop still again / at will / where he wants to."[14] Weigel installed the prototype of this invention in 1670 in his own house, the Domus Weigeliana, which was one of the seven wonders of Jena (see fig. on page 11). In this first version of the "Flying Chair", which was designed for the weight of a specific person, the passenger could let himself up and down (on the right). Almost fifty years later in 1714, the development of the "Flying Chair" was continued by the architectural theorist and master builder Leonhardt Christoph Sturm (1669–1719).[15] Following on from Weigel's invention, Sturm invented two different installations. The first had a crank wheel drive (in the middle), and the second envisaged the use of extra counterweights as a major advance to enable people of different weights to be transported (on the left). In the 18th century, lifts were very popular in the palaces of the nobility, for example the lift in the „Palace of Old Dresden" of August the Strong from 1717 and the lift in Schönbrunn Palace where in 1772, by order of Maria Theresia "an artificial machine" was installed with which "10 and more persons could be transported up and down through the storeys by a single wheel which is operated by a single person."[16]

But the real breakthrough for the passenger lift was achieved in the middle of the 19th century by Elisha Graves Otis (1811–1861). In 1852 he developed the safety hoist – the first lift which was fitted with an automatic safety device. With this mechanism, which arrests the lift cabin on toothed guide rails with the aid of a pre-tensioned cabin spring to prevent it from falling when it becomes too fast or the suspension gear breaks, Elisha Graves Otis paved the way for modern lift construction. The new feature, according to Otis in the patent documents, was that the stopping "is made to be automati-

den sieben Wundern Jenas zählte (rechte Darstellung in der Abbildung). Bei dieser ersten Art des »Fliegenden Stuhles«, der noch auf das Gewicht einer bestimmten Person ausgerichtet war, konnte sich der Fahrgast selbst hoch- und niederlassen. Knapp fünfzig Jahre später, 1714, wurde die Entwicklung des »Fliegenden Stuhles« weitergeführt durch den Architekturtheoretiker und Baumeister Leonhardt Christoph Sturm (1669–1719).[15] In Fortsetzung von Weigels Erfindung konzipierte Sturm zwei unterschiedliche Anlagen: die erste sah einen Kurbelantrieb vor (mittlere Darstellung in der Abbildung) und die zweite durch die Verwendung zusätzlicher Gegengewichte als wesentlichen Fortschritt die Möglichkeit des Transportes von Personen unterschiedlichen Gewichtes (linke Darstellung in der Abbildung). Für den großen Zuspruch, den der Fahrstuhl im 18. Jahrhundert in Adelspalästen fand, werden hier beispielhaft die Anlagen im »Palais zu Alt-Dreßden« von August dem Starken von 1717 und in Schloß Schönbrunn genannt, in dem 1772 auf Veranlassung von Maria Theresia »eine künstliche Maschine« installiert wurde, durch die »10 und mehr Personen durch die Stockwerke durch ein einziges Rad, welches von einem Menschen getrieben wird, auf und ab bewegt« wurden.[16]

Den eigentlichen Durchbruch erlebte der Personenaufzug jedoch erst Mitte des 19. Jahrhunderts mit Elisha Graves Otis (1811–1861), der 1852 den *safety hoist* entwickelte – den ersten Aufzug, der mit einer automatischen Fangvorrichtung ausgestattet war. Mit diesem Mechanismus, der den Fahrkorb an ge-

Drei Varianten des »Fliegenden Stuhles« von Erhard Weigel und Leonhardt Christoph Sturm, Augsburg 1714

Three versions of the "Flying Chair" by Erhard Weigel and Leonhardt Christoph Sturm, Augsburg, 1714

zahnten Führungsschienen mit Hilfe einer vorgespannten Wagenfeder bei Übergeschwindigkeit oder Bruch der Tragmittel arretiert und gegen Absturz sichert, ebnete Elisha Graves Otis den Weg für den modernen Aufzugsbau. Das Novum bestand darin, daß die Abstoppung, so Otis in der Patentschrift, »is made to be automatically and simultaneously« – im Gegensatz zu den früheren, vorwiegend dem Gütertransport dienenden Aufzügen, die entweder keine Notbremse hatten oder eine, die von Hand betätigt werden mußte. Im Jahr 1853 präsentierte Otis seine Erfindung auf der internationalen Ausstellung im New Yorker Chrystal Palace mit den Worten »All safe, Gentlemen, all safe!«. Vier Jahre später wurde in dem fünfgeschossigen E.V. Haughwout-Building in New York der erste dampfbetriebene Personen-Aufzug installiert.[17]

Neben dem durch reine Muskelkraft betriebenen Handaufzug, der bereits erwähnt wurde, existieren als weitere Energiequellen für den Antrieb von Aufzügen Dampf- und Gasmaschinen, Wasserkraft und Elektroenergie.

Eines der frühesten Antriebsysteme ist die auch heute noch weit verbreitete Hydraulik. Bei den ersten Aufzügen dieser Art nutzte man den vorhandenen Wasserdruck zum Heben von Personen und Gütern, während die Abwärtsbewegung durch das Kabineneigengewicht entstand. Zu unterscheiden ist zwischen direktem und indirektem Hydraulik-Antrieb: Bei ersterem ist der Hydraulikkolben mit der Kabine fest verbunden, bei letzterem vermitteln Seile mit Umlenkrollen zwischen Hydraulikkolben und Kabine. Diese

1853 präsentiert Elisha Graves Otis in New York die erste Fangvorrichtung

Elisha Graves Otis presents the first safety gear in New York in 1853

cally and simultaneously" – by contrast with the earlier lifts which were mainly used for goods transport and either had no emergency brake at all, or one which had to be operated by hand. In 1853 Otis presented his invention at the international exhibition in the Crystal Palace in New York with the words: "All safe, gentlemen, all safe!" . Four years later, the first steam-operated passenger lift was installed in the five-storey E.V. Haughwout Building in New York.[17]

Apart from the hand lift operated entirely by muscle power which has already been mentioned, the other possible sources of energy for lifts are steam and gas machines, water power and electricity.

One of the earliest drive systems was hydraulic power, which is still widely used today. In the first lifts of this type, water power was used to raise persons and goods, and the intrinsic weight of the cabin was used for downwards movement. A distinction must be made between direct and indirect hydraulic drives. In the former type the hydraulic piston is firmly connected to the cabin, in the latter type, ropes with pulleys are arranged between the hydraulic piston and the cabin. This method – like all cabins suspended on ropes – requires that safety gear must be fitted to prevent the cabin from falling. After the urban pressurised water supply was initially used, the number of private pumping stations to maintain a constant water pressure increased considerably until, among other negative effects, the first signs of corrosion by the water became apparent. Many lifts of this type were installed in Berlin around the turn of the century, but towards the end of the 1920s they were converted into drum lifts with ropes and electrical drives, as can be seen in the inspection books of the Technical Control Board.

Since the Second World War, oil has been used for hydraulic drives in conjunction with electrically operated pumps because these lift installations take less space, and it is easier to accommodate the machinery room. About 50–60% of all newly installed modern lifts contain this drive system. In the USA, consideration is being given to a possible return to water hydraulics in order to prevent possible contamination from ruptured oil tanks or oil pipes in earthquake areas such as California.

A further technique from the early days of lift construction was the transmission lift in which the transmission shaft was powered by a central steam or gas machine. This system was mainly used in factories because it was only suitable for use within buildings.

In the early lifts in Berlin we often find drum lifts, which are only rarely installed today. The ropes on which the cabins hang are wound onto a drum as the cabin travels upwards, which limits the possible travel height. A counterweight can be used to save energy, and it was often accommodated in a separate shaft. This permitted a larger cabin to be used even in a narrow stair well. Drum lifts were powered by water power, steam or gas machines, and later by electric motors.

A further possible method of vertical transport is the so-called climbing lift with a cabin sup-

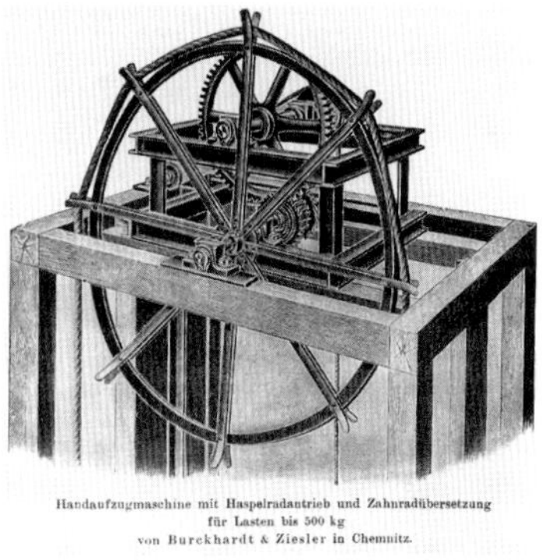

Handaufzugmaschine mit Haspelradantrieb und Zahnradübersetzung für Lasten bis 500 kg von Burckhardt & Ziesler in Chemnitz

Hand hoisting machine powered by a chain pulley with toothed wheel transmission for loads up to 500 kg by Burckhardt & Ziesler in Chemnitz

Methode erfordert – wie bei allen Kabinen, die an Seilen aufgehängt werden – den Einbau einer Fangvorrichtung zur Verhinderung eines Kabinenabsturzes. Nachdem zunächst städtisches Druckwasser genutzt wurde, nahm zur Wahrung eines kontinuierlichen Wasserdrucks die Anzahl privater Pumpstationen bald deutlich zu, bis sich neben anderen negativen Begleiterscheinungen erste Korrosionen durch das Wasser zeigten. In Berlin wurden um die Jahrhundertwende zahlreiche Aufzüge dieser Art installiert, die man gegen Ende der 1920er Jahre jedoch in Trommel-Aufzüge mit Seilen und Elektroantrieb umwandelte, wie die Untersuchungsbücher des Technischen Überwachungs-Vereins zeigen.

Seit dem Zweiten Weltkrieg wird für Hydraulikantriebe in Verbindung mit elektrisch angetriebenen Pumpen Öl anstelle von Wasser verwendet, da solche Aufzugsanlagen weniger Raum beanspruchen und der Maschinenraum leichter unterzubringen ist. Etwa 50–60% aller neu installierten Aufzüge erhalten in heute dieses Antriebsystem. In den USA reifen derzeitig Überlegungen hinsichtlich einer Rückkehr zur Wasser-Hydraulik, um in Erdbebengebieten wie Kalifornien möglichen Verunreinigungen durch gebrochene Öltanks oder Ölleitungen vorzubeugen.

Ebenfalls aus den Anfängen des Aufzugsbaues datiert der Transmissions-Aufzug, bei dem die Transmissionswelle durch eine zentrale Dampf- oder Gasmaschine angetrieben wurde. Dieses System fand vor allem in Fabriken Verwendung, da es sich nur zur Nutzung innerhalb eines einzigen Gebäudes eignete.

In den frühen Berliner Anlagen begegnet man sehr häufig Trommel-Aufzügen, die in heutiger Zeit nur noch selten installiert werden. Die Seile, an denen die Kabinen hängen, werden bei der Aufwärtsfahrt auf eine Trommel gewickelt, wodurch sich eine Begrenzung der Förderhöhe ergibt. Zur Energieeinsparung eignet sich die Verwendung eines Gegengewichtes, welches häufig in einem separaten Schacht eingebaut wurde. Das ermöglichte auch in einem engen Treppenhaus die Nutzung einer größeren Kabine. Angetrieben wurden die Trommel-Aufzüge mit Wasserkraft, Dampf- oder Gasmaschinen sowie in späterer Zeit mit Elektromotoren.

Eine weitere Möglichkeit des Vertikaltransportes bieten die sogenannten Kletter-Aufzüge, deren Kabinen von zwei Zahnstangen getragen werden. In der Regel wird unter dem Kabinenboden ein Getriebe mit Elektromotor zum Antrieb der Zahnräder installiert, die in die Zahnstangen greifen und die Kabinen auf- bzw. abwärts bewegen. Diesen ersten elektrisch angetriebenen Aufzug präsentierte Werner von Siemens (1816–1892) im Jahr 1880 auf der Pfalzgau-Ausstellung in Mannheim und überwand dort mit einem 4-PS-Motor und einer Geschwindigkeit von einem halben Meter pro Sekunde eine Höhendifferenz von 20 Metern. Anlaß für diese Konzeption, die ohne Marktakzeptanz blieb, war das fehlende Vertrauen in die Zuverlässigkeit von Seilaufzügen. Heute begegnet uns dieses System erneut in Gestalt temporär installierter, freistehender Bauaufzüge. Bahnbrechend für die Entwicklung der Aufzugsindustrie wurde indes der Antrieb durch Elektromotoren.

Sie bilden auch die Grundlage für die Treibscheiben-Aufzüge, die seit etwa 1904 installiert werden und technisch auf der von Friedrich Koepe (1835–1922) erdachten Treibscheibe basieren, die 1877 im Bergbau eingeführt worden ist. Über eine große Scheibe werden, vergleichbar mit Schlauch und Felge beim

Ein Bauaufzug der Firma Alimak aus heutiger Zeit

A modern Building lift by the Alimak company

ported by two toothed racks. Generally, a gearbox is fitted below the cabin floor with an electrical motor to drive the cog wheels which engage in the toothed racks and move the cabin up or down. This first electrically operated lift was presented in 1880 by Werner von Siemens (1816–1892) at the Pfalzgau exhibition in Mannheim, where it overcame a height difference of 20 metres with its 4 hp motor at a speed of half a metre per second. The origin of this concept, which was not accepted in the market, was the frequent lack of trust in the reliability of rope lifts. Today we again encounter this system in the form of temporarily installed, free-standing building hoists. But the drive mechanism with electrically powered motors set the trend for the development of the lift industry.

These motors also formed the basis for friction-driven lifts which were installed from about 1904 and were based on the technology of the friction drive sheave invented by Friedrich Koepe (1835–1922), which was used in mining from 1877. Steel ropes are laid into grooves on a large sheave, similar to the tube and rim of a bicycle wheel. One of the ends of the rope bears the cabin, the other holds a counterweight to compensate for the weight of the cabin and part of the payload. For small lift transport heights, geared machines with electrical motors are used, and in tall buildings slow-running electrical motors without gears are used. Because of the invention of the safety gear by Elisha Graves Otis and the use of speed limiters, this lift configuration is one of the safest methods of passenger transport in the world and permits any height to be covered – even the *One Mile Tower* which was designed by Frank Lloyd Wright but never built.[18]

Spindle and supporting chain lifts were designed and installed after the turn of the century, especially for short lifting distances. They have not been of any significance at all for passenger transport. In Berlin there are two examples of the spindle system dating from 1957 in residential buildings at Frankfurter Tor. They have wooden cabins and are still in very good condition, fully functional but hardly used (Fig. 79).

Widely differing drive systems have been developed over the last 150 years and now, at last, the "dream of a lift without ropes and pistons" has been realised on an industrial basis and presented to the public in 1997. Similar to the climbing lift of Werner von Siemens, the drive is again mounted under the cabin. The movement of the cabin up and down is achieved by means of friction wheels on guide rails, powered by a geared electric motor. A counterweight is used to reduce the energy consumption, and a safety gear is installed for the safety of the passengers. This product has been introduced to the market under the name SchindlerMobile®.

The terminology used in German has an interesting history. The term *Fahrstuhl*, which was

SchindlerMobile®, der andere Aufzug

SchindlerMobile®, a different kind of lift

Fahrrad, Stahlseile in profilierte Rillen gelegt. Eines der Seilenden trägt die Kabine, das andere ein Gegengewicht zur Kompensation des Kabinengewichtes und eines Teils der Nutzlast. Bei kleineren Förderhöhen werden Getriebemaschinen, verbunden mit Elektromotoren, verwendet, während bei hohen Häusern langsam laufende Elektromotoren ohne Getriebe zum Einsatz kommen. Diese Aufzugskonfigurationen zählen durch die Erfindung der Fangvorrichtung von Elisha Graves Otis in Verbindung mit Geschwindigkeitsbegrenzern zu den sichersten Personentransportmitteln aller Zeiten und ermöglichen die Erschließung jeder Höhe – sogar des von Frank Lloyd Wright entworfenen *One Mile Tower*, der jedoch nicht realisiert wurde.[18]

Speziell für kleine Hubhöhen wurden nach der Jahrhundertwende die Spindel- und Stützketten-Aufzüge konstruiert und installiert. Sie sind grundsätzlich für den Personentransport ohne Bedeutung geblieben. In Berlin existieren zwei Beispiele des Spindelsystems aus dem Jahr 1957 in Wohnhäusern am Frankfurter Tor. Ausgestattet mit Holzkabinen und noch immer in sehr gutem Zustand, sind sie betriebsbereit, aber kaum genutzt (Abb. 79).

Nach 150 Jahren, in denen die unterschiedlichsten Antriebsysteme entwickelt wurden, ist nun schließlich der »Traum vom seil- und kolbenlosen Aufzug« auf industrieller Basis verwirklicht und 1997 der Öffentlichkeit präsentiert worden. Ähnlich wie bei dem Kletter-Aufzug von Werner von Siemens liegt der Antrieb wiederum unter der Kabine. Deren Auf- und Abwärtsbewegung erfolgt durch Reib- oder Hafträder an Führungsschienen, angetrieben durch einen Elektromotor mit Getriebe. Die Nutzung eines Gegengewichtes bewirkt eine Verminderung der Energieaufnahme, und zur Sicherheit der Fahrgäste ist eine Fangvorrichtung installiert. Im Markt eingeführt ist dieses Produkt unter der Bezeichnung »SchindlerMobile®«.

Bleibt noch die Frage der Begriffsbestimmung. Berühmte Filmtitel wie *Fahrstuhl zum Schafott* und *Fahrstuhl des Grauens* prägten den allgemeinen Sprachgebrauch, während der Sachkundige vom Aufzug oder Lift spricht. Der Ausdruck »Fahrstuhl« nimmt Bezug auf die »Fliegenden Stühle« des 17. und 18. Jahrhunderts. Die abklappbaren Sitzbänke oder Einzelsitze, die uns vor allem in Anlagen des ersten Viertels des 20. Jahrhunderts begegnen, unterstützen diese Vorstellung von einem »fahrenden Stuhl« (Abb. 8, 49, 59, 60). Mit dem Terminus »Aufzug« wird statt dessen der technische Vorgang des (Hin-)Aufziehens beschrieben – ebenso wie mit den englischen Bezeichnungen *lift* und *elevator* sowie dem französischen Ausdruck *ascenseur*.

Zuletzt sei hier noch darauf hingewiesen, daß auf Wunsch vieler Hauseigentümer auf genaue Standortangaben verzichtet wird. Die Bildunterschriften konzentrieren sich auf die Angabe von Bezirk, Installationsjahr der Anlage, Herstellungsfirma der Aufzüge, Gebäudegattung und – soweit bekannt – den Architekten des Gebäudes.

Wir danken allen, die uns bei unserem Vorhaben unterstützten: H. Arens, Dr. A. Arnulf, H. Backe, P. Bothe, C. Bründel, H. Droege, M. Fiedler, Dr. G. Fuchs, K. Gareis, H. Glausch, A. Haffert, K. Hendel, G. Horny, R. Janz, H. Joos, J. Kleemann, B. Kühn, J. Kühn, B. Kustos, K. Lackner, Dr. P. Lemburg, C. Ludwig, K. Müller, H.D. Nagel, G. Radicke, Dr. J. Rucki, H.J. Schulz, P. Schulze, Dr. J. Simmen, W. Spieß, K. Strelow, Dr. H. Voltolini, Dr. B. Werche, G. Zucknick, den Firmen Gottschalk & Michaelis GmbH, Otis GmbH, Schindler Aufzügefabrik GmbH sowie Elevator World, Foto Meyer, Liftreport und dem VDMA (Fachgemeinschaft Fördertechnik). Des weiteren gilt unser Dank den Besitzern und Verwaltern der Häuser, in denen sich die abgebildeten Aufzüge befinden.

popularised in a number of films and is still the most frequent term in general use, actually means "travelling chair" and originates from the "flying chairs" of the 17th and 18th centuries. The fold-down benches or single seats, which can be seen especially in lifts from the first quarter of the 20th century, support this concept of a "travelling chair" (Fig. 8, 49, 59, 60).

Technical experts, on the other hand, tend to use the term *Aufzug* or even to borrow the English name *Lift*. *Aufzug* (pull-up) refers to the technical process of upward motion – similar to the English terms *lift* and *elevator* and the French *ascenseur*.

It remains to note that exact details of the locations have been omitted at the request of the building owners. The picture captions concentrate on the name of the urban district, the year of installation, the type of building, the manufacturer of the lift and – where known – the architect of the building.

We express out thanks to all those who have supported us in our project: H. Arens, Dr. A. Arnulf, H. Backe, P. Bothe, C. Bründel, H. Droege, M. Fiedler, Dr. G. Fuchs, K. Gareis, H. Glausch, A. Haffert, K. Hendel, G.Horny, R. Janz, H. Joos, J. Kleemann, B. Kühn, J. Kühn, B. Kustos, K. Lackner, Dr. P. Lemburg, C. Ludwig, K. Müller, H. D. Nagel, G. Radicke, Dr. J. Rucki, H. J. Schulz, P. Schulze, Dr. J. Simmen, W. Spiess, K. Strelow, Dr. H. Voltolini, Dr. B. Werche, G. Zucknick, the manufacturers Gottschalk & Michaelis GmbH, Otis GmbH and Schindler Aufzügefabrik GmbH and also Elevator World, Foto Meyer, Liftreport and the VDMA (Conveyor Technology Association). We also thank the proprietors and managers of the buildings in which the lifts illustrated are situated.

Late Historicism and Art Nouveau

Berlin developed its characteristic 20th century urban structure from about 1890 onwards. At the same time as the development of the inner city, especially the Dorotheenstadt and Friedrichstadt areas, to become a densely structured shopping and administrative district, the westward expansion of the city that began in the second half of the 19th century also continued. This expansion led to the formation of new urban districts for the high and middle class bourgeois.[19] The westward tendency was also reflected in the lift industry. In the early years of the 20th century, a large number of new lifts were installed on Kurfürstendamm and its side streets, on Kaiserdamm, around the Lietzenseepark and in the area with Bavarian street names. But as over 50% of the inner city was destroyed during the Second World War, no detailed information is now available on the design of lifts in this area. Extraordinary architectural solutions in famous hotels and large stores were destroyed during the war. The few remaining examples of the early period of lift construction in the inner city include the recently completely overhauled, splendid portal in a residential and shopping house in Friedrichstadt which dates from 1900 (Fig. 5) and two lifts dating from 1905 (Fig. 11, 12) in Friedrichstadt and Dorotheenstadt.

The pictures of lifts from the first two decades of the 20th century mainly show lift installations in residential buildings. "As early as 1899, 48% of the 52515 buildings on residential land consisted of five (41%), six or seven storeys; 26% had only one or two storeys and a further 26% had three or four storeys (including the ground floor)."[20] But at the beginning of the century lifts were not yet regarded as standard fittings for multi-storey buildings. Often they were only fitted retrospectively into or next to the stair well. If there was insufficient space on the ground floor, access to the cabin was only possible in

Später Historismus und Jugendstil

Seine für das 20. Jahrhundert bestimmenden städtebaulichen Charakteristika bildete Berlin seit etwa 1890 heraus: Gleichzeitig mit der Entwicklung der Innenstadt, insbesondere der Dorotheen- und Friedrichstadt, zum dichten Geschäfts- und Verwaltungsviertel setzte sich die in der zweiten Hälfte des 19. Jahrhunderts begonnene Erweiterung nach Westen fort. Diese führte zur Bildung neuer Stadtviertel für mittlere und gehobene Bürgerschichten.[19] Der Zug nach Westen spiegelt sich auch in der Aufzugsindustrie wider, die im ersten Jahrzehnt unseres Jahrhunderts eine große Anzahl von Neuanlagen in Wohnhäusern auf dem Kurfürstendamm und dessen Seitenstraßen, dem Kaiserdamm mit Lietzenseepark und im Bayerischen Viertel zu verzeichnen hatte. Nachdem die Innenstadt infolge des Zweiten Weltkrieges zu über 50% vernichtet worden ist, sind in heutiger Zeit keine genauen Aussagen zur Gestaltung von Aufzügen in diesem Gebiet mehr möglich. Außergewöhnliche architektonische Lösungen in berühmten Hotels und Kaufhäusern sind während des Krieges zerstört worden. Zu den wenigen erhaltenen, innerstädtischen Beispielen der Frühzeit zählen die in jüngerer Zeit vollständig sanierten, prunkvollen Portale in einem Wohn- und Geschäftshaus des Jahres 1900 in der Friedrichstadt (Abb. 5) sowie zwei Anlagen von 1905 (Abb. 11, 12) in der Friedrich- bzw. der Dorotheenstadt.

Die Bildbeispiele der ersten zwei Jahrzehnte des 20. Jahrhunderts zeigen vorwiegend Aufzugsanlagen in Wohnhäusern: »Schon 1899 bestanden 48% aller 52515 Gebäude auf den Wohngrundstücken aus fünf (41%), sechs oder sieben Geschossen; 26% besaßen nur ein oder zwei Geschosse und ebenfalls 26% besaßen drei oder vier Geschosse (Erdgeschoß eingeschlossen).«[20] Allerdings gehörten Aufzüge zu Beginn unseres

Jahrhunderts noch nicht zur Grundausstattung eines mehrgeschossigen Hauses, sondern wurden – zur Steigerung der Wohnqualität und besseren Vermietbarkeit der oberen Geschosse – häufig erst nachträglich in oder neben das Treppenauge eingebaut. Fehlte der Platz im Erdgeschoß, war die Kabine erst im Hochparterre zugänglich (Abb. 13). Bei Anlagen mit Trommelantrieb wurden die Gegengewichte zuweilen in separaten Schächten untergebracht, um das enge Treppenhaus vollständig für die Kabine nutzbar zu machen (Abb. 26, 31, 37).

Die sofortigen Einbauten unterscheiden sich von den nachträglichen in der Regel durch die einheitliche Gestaltung von Aufzugs- und Wohnungstüren (Abb. 18 und 32), die Integration der Portierslogen in die Aufzugsportale (Abb. 15 und 30) oder die Einbindung der Anlage in die Gesamtkonzeption des Treppenhauses (Abb. 21 und 36). Auch die Einbauten in Mauernischen datieren häufig aus der Entstehungszeit des Hauses (Abb. 19). Interessant ist in diesem Zusammenhang die Beobachtung, daß die Schachtverkleidungen innerhalb eines Hauses differieren können – und zwar nicht nur im Dekor, der zumeist im Erdgeschoß bzw. Hochparterre die reichste Ornamentik aufweist, sondern auch in Gestaltung und Material. Dies zeigt sich in einer Anlage des Jahres 1911 im Bezirk Tiergarten, die im Erdgeschoß allerdings einen außergewöhnlich schlichten Zugang aufweist – verborgen hinter einer großzügigen Treppenanlage. Im Hochparterre findet sich dann ein eisernes Schachtgerüst mit stilisiertem Rosetten- und Rankendekor (Abb. 42). Dessen schlichte Gestaltung steht in deutlichem Kontrast zu den Holzportalen der oberen Stockwerke (Abb. 43), die Bezug nehmen auf die Architektur- und Möbelornamentik der deutschen Renaissancekunst des späten 16. und frühen 17. Jahrhunderts. Sie sind reich verziert und dreizonig im Aufbau: Über einer gegliederten Sockelzone mit hohen, schlanken Postamenten öffnen sich die drei Rundbogenfenster der Aufzugs- und zweiflügeligen Wohnungstür. Die Türen werden flankiert

the intermediate storey (Fig. 13). In lifts with drums, the counterweights were sometimes housed in separate shafts so that the space in the narrow stair well could be used entirely for the cabin (Fig. 26, 31, 37).

Lifts installed in the construction phase were generally distinguished from retrofitted lifts in that there was a uniform design of the lift and flat doors (Fig. 18 and 32), the caretaker's lodges were integrated into the lift portals (Fig. 15 and 30) and the lift formed an integral part of the overall concept of the stair well (Fig. 21 and 36). Lifts fitted into recesses in the wall also often date from the time of origin of the buildings (Fig. 19). In this connection it is interesting to observe that the cladding of the shaft can differ within a single building – not only in the decoration, which is normally most ornamental on the ground floor or intermediate storey above the ground floor, but also in its design and material. This is apparent in a lift dating from 1911 in the district of Tiergarten. This lift has an extremely modest entrance on the ground floor – hidden behind a generously proportioned staircase. In the intermediate storey above the ground floor there is then an iron shaft framework with a stylised rosette and vine decor (Fig. 42). The simple design of this framework is in clear contrast to the wooden portals of the upper storeys (Fig. 43) which make reference to the architectural and furniture ornamentation of German Renaissance art of the late 16th and early 17th century. They are richly decorated and structured in three zones: above a subdivided base zone with high, slender pedestals rise the three round arch windows of the lift door and the two-leaf door to the flat. The doors are flanked by columns with profile bases, ornamental carvings in the lower part of the shaft and leaf capitals which support a smooth architrave and a profiled cornice with a toothed frieze. The upper end of the portal is formed by a recessed five-arch column arcade.

In 1900 Carl Flohr, one of the pioneers of lift construction, characterised the lift as "an adornment of a building": "From the point of view of machinery and artistic craftsmanship, it embodies the highest achievement of lift technology."[21] According to Flohr, the "entrance doors and surrounds were made of the richest wrought ironwork of iron or bronze, designed to match the style of the setting. Wherever you look, the eye beholds dainty lattice work, often ennobled by gold-plating, artistically decorated mirror glass, rich woodwork, ample cushions etc."[22] This description not only mentions the main materials, it also reflects the fact that there was no industrial mass production in the early lift industry. A harmonisation of the decor and design of wrought iron portals and shaft surrounds can be observed in three adjacent buildings dating from 1900 near Kurfürstendamm (Fig. 3 and 4). The wrought iron work was not carried out by the lift companies, it was produced in locksmith craft companies which were responsible for the production and assembly of the ironwork. "Such working hand in hand will be of benefit for all partners involved. The machine manufacturer will not have any great interest in carrying out the ironwork because it can not be done to a pattern, but usually has to be designed, calculated in size and produced in each individual case in accordance with the local conditions."[23] This also applied to the wrought iron cabins, although only very few have been preserved (Fig. 4, 6, 16).

Stylistically, the forms of the lifts that were installed up to the middle of the second decade corresponded either to late Historicism or to the style of the Art Nouveau. The term Historicism as a concept in art history first appeared in 1929 in *Wasmuth's lexicon of architecture* to characterise the architectural period between Classicism and Art Nouveau. Stylistic references to previous epochs created a number of revived styles such as "New Gothic", "New Romanticism", "New Renaissance", "New Baroque" and "New Classicism", which the architectural critic Adolf Behne (1895–1948) called "conserved" styles.[24] In an "attempt to define the concept" in 1970, Wolfgang Götz distinguished between Historicism as a way of thinking and Eclecticism (Greek *eklegein*

von Säulen mit profilierten Basen, ornamentalem Schnitzwerk im unteren Schaftbereich und Blattkapitellen, die einen glatten Architrav und ein profiliertes Gesims mit Zahnschnittfries tragen. Den oberen Portalabschluß bildet eine zurückgesetzte fünfbogige Säulenarkade.

Carl Flohr, einer der Pioniere des Aufzugsbaues, charakterisierte im Jahr 1900 den Aufzug als »ein Prachtstück des Hauses«: »In ihm ist nach maschinentechnischer und kunstgewerblicher Seite die höchste Leistung der Aufzugstechnik verkörpert.«[21] Nach Flohr wurden die »Zugangsthüren und Umwährungen [sic!] in reichster Kunstschmiedearbeit aus Eisen oder Bronze, dem Stil der Umgebung angepaßt, ausgeführt. Wohin man schaut, sieht das Auge zierliches Gitterwerk, oft durch Vergoldungen gehoben, kunstvoll verziertes Spiegelglas, reiches Holzwerk, schwellende Polster usw.«[22] Damit sind nicht nur die wesentlichen Materialien genannt, sondern wird auch der Tatsache Ausdruck gegeben, daß in der Aufzugsindustrie der frühen Zeit keine industrielle Fertigung stattfand. Übereinstimmungen in Dekor und Ausführung von schmiedeeisernem Portal und Schachtumwehrung finden in drei benachbarten Häusern aus dem Jahre 1900 nahe dem Kurfürstendamm (Abb. 3 und 4). Die Kunstschmiedearbeiten wurden nicht von den Aufzugsfirmen, sondern in Kunstschlossereien hergestellt, denen Ausführung und Montage der Eisenkonstruktionen oblag: »Ein solches Handinhandarbeiten wird allen beteiligten Faktoren von Nutzen sein. Der Maschinenfabrikant wird wenig darnach [sic!] streben, auch die Eisenkonstruktion auszuführen, da sie ja nicht schablonenmässig durchgeführt werden können, sondern meist in jedem einzelnen Falle den örtlichen Verhältnissen entsprechend konstruiert, dimensioniert und ausgeführt werden müssen.«[23] Dies gilt auch für die geschmiedeten Kabinen, von denen sich nur wenige erhalten haben (Abb. 4, 6, 16).

Stilistisch entsprechen die Anlagen, die bis zur Mitte des zweiten Jahrzehnts installiert wurden, in ihrer Formensprache entweder dem späten Historismus oder dem Jugendstil. Zuweilen verbinden sich auch Elemente beider Stilrichtungen miteinander. Als Begriff der Kunstgeschichte erscheint der Historismus erstmals 1929 in *Wasmuths Lexikon der Baukunst* zur Charakterisierung der Bauperiode zwischen Klassizismus und Jugendstil. Im stilistischen Rückgriff auf frühere Epochen entstanden die sogenannten Neo-Stile wie »Neugotik«, »Neuromanik«, »Neo-Renaissance«, »Neubarock« und »Neo-Klassizismus«, die der Architekturkritiker Adolf Behne (1895–1948), als »konservierte« Stile bezeichnete.[24] In einem »Versuch zur Definition des Begriffs« unterscheidet Wolfgang Götz 1970 zwischen Historismus als Gesinnung und Eklektizismus (griech. *eklegein* = auswählen) als Methode. Zudem weist er ausdrücklich darauf hin, daß es »ein eklektizistisches Verarbeiten historischer Formvorbilder, ein Zurückgreifen auf alte Stilarten und Stilformen [...] zu allen Zeiten in der abendländischen Kunstgeschichte« gegeben hat.[25]

Das historistische Formenvokabular in der frühen Berliner Aufzugsarchitektur an den Portalen und Schachtumwehrungen umfaßt üppiges Blattwerk in Gestalt von Ranken, Kränzen und Girlanden (z.B. Abb. 4, 10, 31) sowie klassische Elemente wie Palmetten und Mäanderfriese (siehe Frontispiz), Füllhörner (Abb. 22 und 56) und Schuppendekor (Abb. 3). Uns begegnen Supraporten im Stil des Neo-Rokoko in einem Beispiel von 1900 (Abb. 5) ebenso wie Elemente der Neo-Renaissance in einer Anlage von 1908, die mit korinthischen Pilasterkapitellen, Architrav und Giebelmotiv die klassische Architekturornamentik variiert (Abb. 21 und 22). Auch die Flachreliefs der Treppenhauspfeiler mit Lyra- und Masken-Dekor sind motivische Anleihen der Renaissance in diesem Ensemble, das zugleich ein hervorragendes Beispiel einheitlicher Gestaltung von Treppenhaus und Aufzugslobby darstellt (Abb. 21).

Gleichzeitig mit dem Historismus begegnet uns in der Berliner Aufzugsarchitektur der ersten zwei Jahrzehnte der Jugendstil, der begrifflich vom Titel der

= choose) as a method. He also expressly pointed out that there has been "an eclectic processing of historical form models, a reference back to old styles and forms [...] in all periods of western art history."[25]

The range of historical forms in the portals and shaft surrounds in lift architecture in Berlin includes rich foliage in the form of vines, wreaths and garlands (e.g. Fig. 4, 10, 31), classical elements such as palmettes fretwork, cornucopias (Fig. 22 and 56) and scales (Fig. 3). We encounter supraportas in the New Rococo style in an example dating from 1900 (Fig. 5) and New Renaissance elements in a lift of 1908, which varies classical architectural ornamentation with Corinthian pilaster capitals, architrave and gable motifs (Fig. 21 and 22). And the flat reliefs of the staircase columns with a lyre and mask decor are based on Renaissance motifs in this ensemble, which is also an excellent example of the uniform design of the staircase and the lift lobby (Fig. 21).

At the same time as Historicism, we also encounter Art Nouveau in Berlin lift architecture of the first two decades of the 20th century. The German term for this movement, *Jugendstil*, was derived from the title of the periodical *Jugend* (Youth), the first issue of which was published in January 1896. In German usage, *Jugendstil* is used to denote art and fine art forms which arose between 1895 and 1914 in the "modern" style. Its proponents deliberately aimed to break away from the traditions and historical styles of the 19th century and to create a new type of art (French: *Art Nouveau*; English: *Modern style*). "In formal terms, the renewal of applied art was a way of designing surfaces which was inspired by the example of Japan and did not reflect the realistic perspective in portrayals of Nature which was traditional in Europe; instead, it took an unaccustomed perspective on the living, germinating, budding and permanently moving aspects of Nature as the content of its pictures."[26] This can be seen in the earliest lift preserved in Berlin dating from 1899 and in an example from 1902 in which the door decor contains dynamic linear patterns with a few greatly reduced blossoms and buds (Fig. 1 and 6). In addition to these ornamental floral decors, we also encounter various geometric ornaments (Fig. 7, 19, 34). A lift dating from 1906 is remarkable because of the high degree of abstraction in the pattern and the reduction of the colours to black and white, which reminds us of the work of the Viennese workshops[27] (Fig. 15).

As an unusual solution from these early years, the presentation of two peacocks, must be emphasised on a three-zone portal of 1912 in Weißensee (Fig. 45). Above a closed base area subdivided into rectangular panels, the portal opens out to the shaft with lattice work interrupted by spiral forms which is backed by wire mesh. The peacocks stand on the lintel of the portal and surround the shaft door with their long tails which are covered with stylised eyes.

In addition to the shaft surrounds and portals, it is also worth noting the company and information signs , cabin entrance thresholds (Fig. 39 and 64) and especially the tableaux inside and outside the lift for their artistic design. This particularly applies to a cabin tableau of AEG from 1907 which was fitted into a lift in Charlottenburg two years later.[28] The design goes back to Otto Eckmann (1865–1902), one of the most important early proponents of Art Nouveau. Eckmann was commissioned by AEG to design printed material and catalogues for the Paris World Exhibition of 1900, and at around the same time he designed a switch panel for the company with a stop switch and a light switch. The special feature of this frame was that it indicated the light switch symbolically as a sun.[29] The 1907 tableau shown here only differs from the original draft in its rational, simple lettering which replaces Eckmann's individual lettering.

A simplification of decor is also shown in a comparison of two tableaux of the Carl Flohr company in lifts dating from 1908 and 1910 (Fig. 25 and 40). In spite of the similarities in their format and their spatial structure, the two panels differ clearly in their formal language. Whereas the older panel has a frame of dynami-

Zeitschrift *Jugend* abzuleiten ist, deren erstes Heft im Januar 1896 erschien. Im deutschen Sprachgebrauch wird mit Jugendstil jenes Kunstgewerbe bezeichnet, das zwischen 1895 und 1914 in »modernem« Stil entstand. Seine Vertreter wollten bewußt mit den Traditionen und historisierenden Stilen des 19. Jahrhunderts brechen und eine neue Kunst (franz. *art nouveau*), einen modernen Stil (engl. *modern style*) begründen: »In formaler Hinsicht ging es bei der Erneuerung des Kunstgewerbes um eine Kunst der Flächengestaltung, die, vom Vorbild Japans inspiriert, nicht das in Europa traditionelle, perspektivisch korrekte Abbild der Natur wiedergibt, sondern das Lebendige, Keimende, Sprießende und sich permanent Bewegende in der Natur aus ungewöhnlicher Perspektive zum Bildinhalt machte.«[26] Entsprechendes findet sich bei dem frühesten, in Berlin erhaltenen Personenaufzug aus dem Jahr 1899 sowie einem Beispiel von 1902, deren Türdekore dynamisch bewegte Lineamente mit wenigen, stark reduzierten Blütenkelchen bzw. Knospen zeigen (Abb. 1 und 6). Neben diesen ornamental-floralen Dekoren begegnen uns auch verschiedene geometrische Ornamente (Abb. 7, 19, 34). Beachtenswert ist dabei eine Anlage von 1906 aufgrund des hohen Abstraktionsgrades in der Musterung und der auf Schwarz und Weiß reduzierten Farbigkeit, die an Arbeiten aus den Wiener Werkstätten[27] denken läßt (Abb. 15).

Als außergewöhnliche Lösung dieser frühen Jahre ist hier vor allem die Darstellung eines Pfauenpaares auf einem dreizonigen Portal von 1912 in Weißensee hervorzuheben (Abb. 45). Über einer durch Rechteckfelder gegliederten, geschlossenen Sockelzone öffnet sich das Portal zum Schacht mit einem von Spiralformen durchbrochenen Gitterwerk, das hinterfangen wird von dichtem Maschendraht. Die Pfauen stehen auf dem Portalsturz und rahmen die Schachttür mit ihren langen Schweifen, die von stilisierten Augenflecken bedeckt werden.

Neben Schachtumwehrungen und Portalen sind aber auch Firmen- und Hinweisschilder, Kabinenantrittschwellen (Abb. 39 und 64) sowie vor allem Tableaus im Innen- und Außenbereich des Aufzuges aufgrund ihrer künstlerischen Gestaltung zu betrachten. Dies gilt insbesondere für ein Kabinentableau des Jahres 1907 von der AEG, das zwei Jahre später in einem Aufzug in Charlottenburg eingesetzt wurde (Abb. 28).[28] Der Entwurf geht zurück auf Otto Eckmann (1865–1902), einen der bedeutendsten Vertreter des frühen Jugendstils. Eckmann wurde von der AEG mit der Gestaltung von Drucksachen und Katalogen zur Pariser Weltausstellung 1900 beauftragt und entwarf für das Unternehmen etwa zur gleichen Zeit eine Schalterrahmung mit Halt- und Lichtschalter, deren Besonderheit in der symbolischen Darstellung des Lichtschalters als Sonne liegt.[29] Das hier abgebildete Tableau von 1907 unterscheidet sich von dem ursprünglichen Entwurf nur durch den sachlich schlichten Schriftzug, der Eckmanns individuelle Schriftform ablöste.

Eine Vereinfachung des Dekors zeigt sich auch im Vergleich zweier Tableaus der Firma Carl Flohr (Abb. 25 und 40) in Aufzügen der Jahre 1908 und 1910. Trotz der Analogien in Format und Oberflächengliederung unterscheiden sich die beiden Tafeln deutlich in ihrer Formensprache: Während das ältere Stück eine Rahmung aus dynamisch geschwungenem Blattwerk und eine runde, ausschwingende Versalschrift aufweist, ist das jüngere Tableau klar und einfach in Aufbau und Ausdruck – mit einer Rahmung aus doppelter Linie unterschiedlicher Stärke und einem unverzierten, blockhaften Schriftzug. Auch das Design der Firma

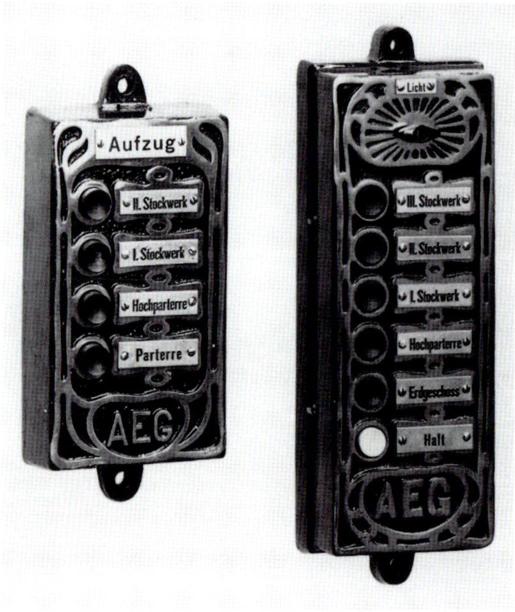

Druckknopfsteuerungen der AEG, 1907

Push-button controls by AEG, 1907

cally curved foliage and rounded, looping capital letters, the later tableau is clear and simple in its structure and expression – with a frame consisting of a double line with different thicknesses and plain, block-type lettering. The design of the Schindler company also developed within a few years from the style of Art Nouveau to Functionalism (Fig. 54 and 55). The unusual monogram of Otis in a 1914 lift is a rarity in which the letters of the name are designed as interlinking capitals.

The lift industry expanded particularly in the years leading up to the Second World War. Whereas there were only four lift companies in Berlin in 1880, there were already fourteen companies eight years later, and in 1893 there were twenty. By the Second World War the number increased to over forty, and today over sixty German and foreign lift companies are registered in the city, and a further 30 companies are represented with products. Four companies founded in the early years remain in existence even today. These companies are Flohr, Gottschalk & Michaelis, Otis and Schindler. In 1879 Carl Flohr(1850–1927) took over a company for milling and crushing equipment from Theodor Lissmann, and this company subsequently produced passenger and goods lifts, hoists and cranes. Only one year after Flohr, Gottschalk & Michaelis founded their company. The Otis Elevator Company founded by Elisha Graves Otis (1811–1861) took up its

Otis-Monogramm, 1914

Otis monogram, 1914

activities in Berlin in 1893 at the latest, and in 1910 it built its first production site in the city. The two companies Flohr and Otis merged in 1951 as Flohr Otis GmbH, and this company has been registered as Otis GmbH since 1993. In 1906, the Swiss firm of Schindler & Cie., which had been founded in Lucerne in 1874 by Robert Schindler (1850–1920), also founded a subsidiary company in Berlin-Tempelhof. This first step was followed in 1911 by the takeover of the Severin Senator company, which was renamed fifteen years later as Schindler Aufzügefabrik GmbH (Schindler lift factory).

Ruftableau von Schindler, um 1910

Lift call panel by Schindler, around 1910

Anzeige der Firma Lißmann (Inhaber Gebrüder Flohr) von 1884

Advertisement by the Lißmann company (proprietor: Flohr Brothers) from 1884

Schindler vollzieht innerhalb weniger Jahre den Wandel vom Jugendstil (siehe nebenstehende Abb.) zur Sachlichkeit (Abb. 54 und 55). Eine Rarität stellt das außergewöhnliche Monogramm von Otis in einem Aufzug von 1914 dar, in dem die Buchstaben des Firmennamens als ineinandergreifende Versalien gestaltet sind (Abb. S. 22).

Die Aufzugsbranche expandierte insbesondere in den Jahren bis zum Zweiten Weltkrieg: Waren es 1880 nur vier Aufzugsunternehmen in Berlin, existierten acht Jahre später bereits vierzehn und 1893 zwanzig Firmen. Bis zum Zweiten Weltkrieg erhöhte sich die Zahl auf über vierzig, und heute sind in dieser Stadt über sechzig in- und ausländische Aufzugshersteller niedergelassen und darüber hinaus etwa weitere dreißig Firmen mit Produkten vertreten.

Vier Gründungen der frühen Jahre haben sich bis heute erhalten. Es handelt sich hierbei um Flohr, Gottschalk & Michaelis, Otis und Schindler. Carl Flohr (1850–1927) übernahm im Jahr 1879 von Theodor Lißmann ein Unternehmen für Mühlen- und Zerkleinerungsanlagen, das in der Folgezeit Personen- und Lastenaufzüge sowie Winden und Kräne produzierte . Nur ein Jahr nach Flohr eröffneten Gottschalk & Michaelis ihr Unternehmen. Die von Elisha Graves Otis (1811–1861) gegründete Otis Elevator Company wurde spätestens 1893 in Berlin tätig und errichtete 1910 ihre erste Produktionsstätte in dieser Stadt. 1951 fusionierten die Unternehmen Flohr und Otis zur Flohr Otis GmbH, die seit 1993 unter Otis GmbH firmiert. 1906 errichtete auch die 1874 durch Robert Schindler (1850–1920) in Luzern gegründete Schweizer Firma Schindler & Cie. eine Tochtergesellschaft in Berlin-Tempelhof. Diesem ersten Schritt folgte 1911 die Übernahme der Firma Severin Senator, die fünfzehn Jahre später in Schindler Aufzügefabrik GmbH umbenannt wurde.

Charlottenburg
1899 • Stigler
Wohnhaus
residential building

1

Charlottenburg
1900 • Stigler
A. Thees:
Wohnhaus
residential building

2

Charlottenburg
1900 • Flohr
Wohnhaus
residential building

4

Transparente
Schachtumwehrung
transparent shaft surround

3

5

Mitte
um 1900
C. Gause:
Wohn- und
Geschäftshaus
residential building
and business centre

6

Charlottenburg
1902 • Neumann & Rechlin
Wohnhaus
residential building

Charlottenburg
1902 • Flohr
Wohnhaus
residential building

7

8

Kabine
cabin

Mitte
1905
Bürogebäude
office building

9

Charlottenburg
1903 • Stigler
Wohnhaus
residential building

Charlottenburg
1903 • Flohr
Wohnhaus
residential building

10

12

Mitte
1905 • Flohr
Universität
university

13

Wilmersdorf
1906 • Stigler
O. Schmock:
Wohnhaus
residential building

Wilmersdorf
1906 • Flohr
Wohnhaus
residential building

14

Charlottenburg
1906 • Berlin-Anhaltin.-
Maschinenb.-A.G.
A. Gessner:
Wohnhaus
residential building

15

Firmenschild
company sign

17

Schöneberg
1906 • Kühnscherf
Wohnhaus
residential building

16

Charlottenburg
1907 • Flohr
Wohnhaus
residential building

Charlottenburg
1907 • Schindler
Wohnhaus
residential building

Kreuzberg
1908 • Piechatzek
Gewerbehof
trade centre

Charlottenburg
1908 • Tenner
Wohnhaus
residential building

21

Obere Haltestelle
upper stop

22

Standortanzeiger
position indicator

23

Wilmersdorf
1908 • Flohr
Wohnhaus
residential building

Kabinentableau
cabin control panel

Charlottenburg
1909 • Gebauer
Wohnhaus
residential building

26

Kabinenansicht
view of cabin

27

Kabinentableau
cabin control panel

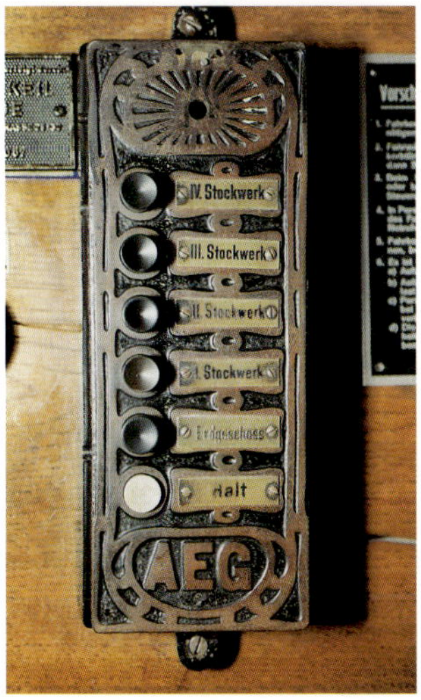

28

Bitte
Fahrstuhl-Tür
leise schließen

Charlottenburg
1909 • Flohr
Wohnhaus
residential building

Charlottenburg
1910 • Kühnscherf
Wohnhaus
residential building

Charlottenburg
1910 • Flohr
Wohnhaus
residential building

Wilmersdorf
1910 • Schindler
Wohnhaus
residential building

Wilmersdorf
1910
Wohnhaus
residential building

32

34

33

Firmenschild
company sign

Schöneberg
1910 • Tenner
Wohnhaus
residential building

35

Charlottenburg
1910 • Tenner
Wohnhaus
residential building

36

Schöneberg
1910 • Schindler
G. Johanson,
P. Wiesener:
Wohnhaus
residential building

Transparente
Schachtumwehrung
transparent shaft surround

Kabinen-
antrittsschwelle
cabin entrance threshold

Wilmersdorf
1910 • Flohr
A. Haase:
Wohnhaus
residential building

Mitte
1910 • Flohr
Bürogebäude
Kabinentableau
office building
cabin control panel

Tiergarten
1911 • Flohr
Wohnhaus
Aufzugsschacht
im Hochparterre
residential building
lift shaft in the
raised ground floor

Portal mit
Wohnungseingang
und Aufzugstür
portal with flat
entrance and lift door

43

Aufzugseingang
entrance to the lift

44

Weißensee
1912 • Fleischmann
Wohnhaus
residential building

Wilmersdorf
1912 • Flohr
Wohnhaus
residential building

Wilmersdorf
1912 • Stigler
Wohnhaus
residential building

Wilmersdorf
1913 • Flohr
Wohnhaus
residential building

Kabine mit
abklappbaren Sitzen
cabin with
fold-down seats

Wilmersdorf
1913
Wohnhaus
residential building

50

Tempelhof
1913 • Fesca
Wohnhaus
Kabinentableau
residential building
cabin control panel

51

Tiergarten
1913 • Flohr
P. Karchow:
Bürogebäude
office building

Charlottenburg
1914 • Schindler
Wohnhaus
residential building

53

Kabinentableau
cabin control panel

54

55

Außenruftableau
external call panel

Mitte
1914 • Flohr
Bürogebäude
office building

Wilmersdorf
1916 • Flohr
M. Welsch:
Wohnhaus
residential building

Wilmersdorf
1916 • Tenner
Wohnhaus
residential building

Kabine mit
abklappbarer Sitzbank
cabin with
fold-down seats

Neue Sachlichkeit

»Die neue Schönheit ist die Schönheit der Sache selbst.« So charakterisierte 1927 Adolf Behne, der führende Architekturkritiker der Weimarer Zeit, kurz und prägnant das ›Neue‹ der Neuen Sachlichkeit: »Sehr im Irrtum sind [...] jene, die unter Sachlichkeit nur Trokkenheit, Schlichtheit und irgend ein mageres Schema verstehen. Sachlichkeit bedeutet verantwortetes Denken, bedeutet ein Schaffen, das alle Zwecke mit und aus der Phantasie erfüllt.«[30]

Geprägt wurde der Begriff der »Neuen Sachlichkeit« Mitte der zwanziger Jahre im Kontext einer Ausstellung der Städtischen Kunsthalle Mannheim durch deren Direktor G.F. Hartlaub.[31] Er bezeichnete damit einen sozialkritisch engagierten Realismus in der Malerei, den insbesondere scharfe Beobachtung und überdeutliche Zeichnung charakterisieren. Zugleich fand der Begriff aber auch Verwendung in der deutschen Architekturdiskussion der zwanziger und beginnenden dreißiger Jahre für die strenge, kubische Architektur des »Neuen Bauens«: »Das Fehlen jeglichen Ornaments ist äußerlich das auffallendste und am meisten in die Augen springende Kennzeichen der neuen Architektur.«[32]

Dies bestätigt die reduzierte Formensprache und Formenstrenge auch in der Aufzugsarchitektur jener Zeit, die uns unter anderem in Bauwerken von Max Taut, Peter Behrens, Hans Scharoun und Otto Firle begegnet. Bei der Frage nach den Urhebern der Aufzugsentwürfe mangelt es leider häufig an den entsprechenden Informationen, da die Aufzüge in der Fachliteratur nur selten Beachtung finden. Eine Ausnahme bildet die Anlage im ehemaligen Verbandshaus der Deutschen Buchdrukker aus der Mitte der zwanziger Jahre, zu der die Äußerung des Bauhistorikers

Ein Slogan der zwanziger Jahre

An advertising slogan from the 1920s

New Functionalism

"The new beauty is the beauty of the object itself." With these words Adolph Behne, the leading architectural critic of the Weimar period, succinctly and aptly described the "newness" of New Functionalism in 1927: "Very much in error are [...] all those who take Functionalism to stand for dryness, simplicity and some form of planned drabness. Functionalism means responsible thinking, creativity which fulfils all purposes with and out of the imagination.[30]

The term *Neue Sachlichkeit* (New Functionalism) was coined in the middle of the 1920s in the context of an exhibition in the Städtische Kunsthalle (town art museum) of Mannheim by the director of the museum, G. F. Hartlaub.[31] He used the term to denote a committed and socially critical realism in painting which was especially characterised by keen observation and a heightened clarity in the drawing technique. At the same time, however, the term was also used in the German architectural discussion of the 1920s and the beginning of the 1930s for the strict, cubic architecture of "new building": "The lack of any ornament is the most striking external feature, and the most noticeable element of the new architecture."[32]

This is also confirmed by the reduced language and strictness of forms in lift architecture of the period which we encounter, among others, in buildings by Max Taut, Peter Behrens, Hans Scharoun and Otto Firle. Unfortunately, we often do not have the necessary information to determine who designed the lifts because they were only rarely mentioned in the specialist literature. An exception is the lift in the former association building of the German book printers dating from the middle of the 1920s, concerning which the building historian Julius Posener is said to have claimed that Max Taut was proud of this lift for the rest of his life.[33] Max Taut was born in 1884 in Königsberg (and died in 1967). In 1911 he founded his own architectural office in Berlin, and in 1914 he set up a joint office with his brother Bruno Taut and Bruno's partner Franz Hoffmann. In the 1920s he built for the German trades union association, the cooperative associations and the association of German book printers. For the latter he designed a complex of buildings in Kreuzberg in the style of old industrial courtyards. Around an almost square courtyard there are a flat roofed residential building of five storeys, two low side wings and a five storey printing works building, with two staircases in front of it on both sides (Fig. 61).[34] The residential building facing the street is a brick building with yellow facing bricks, and its block-type facade is horizontally subdivided with deep loggias and slightly protruding, glazed winter gardens. The two staircases in this building have no lifts. The printing building is a reinforced concrete skeleton structure with visible framework of hammered concrete. The main entrance to this building, which contains workshops, meeting rooms, shop and office rooms, lies in the staircase on the right which contains a glazed lift shaft. The corresponding staircase on the other side of the courtyard contains an auxiliary staircase without a lift.

Both the lift shaft and the cabin have a framework of burnished brass into which rectangular clear glass panels of different sizes are set.[35] The transparency which makes technical equipment such as ropes, guide rails, safety gear and electrical connections visible (Fig. 60) was an expression of the "technicisation" of the period.[36] When the building was built and

Julius Posener überliefert ist, daß Max Taut Zeit seines Lebens stolz auf diesen Aufzug gewesen sei.[33]

Der 1884 in Königsberg geborene Max Taut (gest. 1967), der 1911 ein eigenes Architekturbüro in Berlin gründete und sich 1914 mit seinem Bruder Bruno Taut und dessen Partner Franz Hoffmann zusammenschloß, baute in den zwanziger Jahren für den Allgemeinen Deutschen Gewerkschaftsbund, die Genossenschaften und den Verband der deutschen Buchdrucker. Für letzteren entwarf er in Kreuzberg einen Gebäudekomplex in der Art alter Industriehöfe: Um einen nahezu quadratischen Hof gliedern sich ein flach gedecktes Wohnhaus mit fünf Geschossen, zwei niedrige Seitenflügel sowie ein ebenfalls fünfgeschossiges Druckereigebäude, dem zu beiden Seiten zwei Treppenhäuser vorgelagert sind (Abb. 61).[34] Das zur Straße gelegene Wohnhaus ist ein mit gelben Klinkern verblendeter Mauerwerksbau, dessen blockhafte Fassade horizontal durch tiefe Loggien und leicht vorspringende verglaste Lauben gegliedert ist. Die beiden Treppenhäuser in diesem Haus sind ohne Aufzüge. Bei dem Druckereigebäude handelt es sich um eine Eisenbetonskelettkonstruktion mit sichtbarer Rahmung aus scharriertem Beton. Der Hauptzugang zu diesem Gebäude, in dem sich Werkstätten, Sitzungssäle sowie Geschäfts- und Büroräume befanden, liegt in dem Treppenhaus auf der rechten Seite, durch das ein gläserner Aufzugsschacht führt. Das Pendant auf der gegenüberliegenden Hofseite enthält eine Nebentreppe ohne Fahrstuhl.

Sowohl der Aufzugsschacht als auch die Kabine weisen ein Gerüst aus bruniertem Messing auf, in das rechteckige Klarglasscheiben unterschiedlicher Größe eingesetzt sind.[35] Die Transparenz, die Teile der Technik wie Seile, Führungsschienen, Fangvorrichtung und elektrische Verbindungen sichtbar werden läßt (Abb. 60), ist Ausdruck der »Technifizierung« jener Zeit.[36] Durch die großflächige Verglasung des Treppenhauses in den oberen Stockwerken konnte

GOTTSCHALK MICHAELIS

Eine der frühen Firmen, die noch heute existiert

One of the early companies that still exist today

man zur Entstehungszeit des Hauses, als die Nachbargrundstücke noch unbebaut waren, vom Aufzug aus über den Hof auf die Umgebung blicken. In der einheitlichen Gestaltung des Treppenhauses spiegelt sich die von Julius Posener bestätigte Urheberschaft von Max Taut für diesen Entwurf wider: Analog zur Umwehrung ist das Treppengeländer in bruniertem Messing gearbeitet. Zudem wird die strenge Gliederung des Aufzugsschachtes aufgenommen von der geometrischen Musterung der Wandfliesen in schwarz, rot und gelb, von denen letztere farblich und motivisch die schlanken Neonröhren am Aufzugschacht aufgreifen, mit denen das Treppenhaus beleuchtet wird.[37]

Wenngleich schlichter in der Ausführung, zeichnete sich auch der Eingangsbereich des Bürohauses des Allgemeinen Deutschen Gewerkschaftsbundes durch seine einheitliche Konzeption aus. Das Gebäude entstand 1922–1923 in Berlin-Mitte ebenfalls nach Entwürfen von Max Taut. Für den Aufzugsschacht wurde Maschendraht statt Klarglas verwendet. Nach dem Krieg zunächst restauriert und rekonstruiert, wurde die Umwehrung in jüngster Zeit durch eine Konstruktion aus Stahl und Mattglas ersetzt. Deren Entwurf greift zwar Elemente der ursprünglichen Aufzugsarchitektur auf, ohne diese jedoch im Stil der damaligen Zeit umzusetzen. Bei der heutigen Kabine handelt es sich um ein Serienprodukt.

Das Verwaltungsgebäude der Gewerkschaften von Max Taut aus den Jahren 1922/23 – die Eingangshalle im ursprünglichen Zustand

The administrative building of the trades unnions by Max Taut of 1922/23 – the entrance hall in its original condition

the neighbouring plots were still undeveloped, the large windows of the staircase in the upper storeys meant that it was possible to look from the lift across the courtyard into the surrounding area. The uniform design of the staircase reflects the work of Max Taut as the designer, which is confirmed by Julius Posener. Similar to the lift surround, the stair banister is also made of burnished brass. Moreover, the strict subdivision of the lift shaft also corresponds to the geometrical pattern of the black, red and yellow wall tiles, with the yellow tiles reflecting the colour and form of the narrow neon tubes on the lift shaft which light the staircase.[37]

Although it is plainer in its execution, the entrance to the office building of the German trades union association is also characterised by its coherent design concept. The building was built in Berlin-Mitte in 1922–1923, again to designs by Max Taut. Wire mesh was used for the lift shaft instead of clear glass. Restored and reconstructed after the War, the lift surround has recently been replaced by a steel and matt glass structure. The design of this structure relates to elements of the original lift architecture, but it does not execute them in the style of the period. The present cabin is a mass-produced product.

The facade, staircase and floor plan design in the buildings of Behrens, Scharoun and Firle also enable conclusions to be drawn about the person who designed the lift architecture – in spite of the lack of written sources. One of the late works of Peter Behrens (1868–1940), which was built in 1930 in Charlottenburg-Westend, was a two wing apartment building, which is a steel frame structure with enclosed brickwork in a four to five storey building at the end of a block (Fig. 68).[38] The corner of the building is accentuated by a round bay, which is matched on the courtyard side by the semi-circular protruding staircase. This staircase has a large matt glass surface on the wall side and at the top. The lift shaft in the staircase well contains high light shafts secured with wire mesh so that the cabin is lit by daylight in addition to artificial light (Fig. 66 and 67). The fact that the staircase and lift shaft formally reflect the architecture of the building supports the assumption that Peter Behrens was responsible for the overall design.

The situation is different for the six storey apartment building which was built in 1929–1930 on Hohenzollerndamm in Wilmersdorf (Fig. 65)[39] to plans by the architect Hans Scharoun (1893–1972). Designed as a "bachelors' house", it contains – like the apartment building on Kaiserdamm completed shortly before it[40] – one-room and two-room apartments which vary in size on Hohenzollerndamm from 35 m² to 75 m². "The building block", according to the architect's own description, "consists [...] of two parallel rows separated by the skylight courtyards and staircases, with storeys that are offset against each other by half a storey. Although each storey has six apartments facing onto the staircase, the staggered height of the entrace doors avoids the impression of rented barracks."[41] There are a total of four staircases, three of which are fitted with lifts (Fig. 63). The staircases are similar in their floor plan and design. Characteristic elements of the period are the coloured design of the stair banisters with a red handrail and blue bars and the reduced, geometrical decor of the shaft doors. This reflects

Fassaden-, Treppenhaus- und Grundrißgestaltung in den Gebäuden von Behrens, Scharoun und Firle ermöglichen auch dort – trotz fehlender Schriftquellen und mündlicher Hinweise – Rückschlüsse hinsichtlich der Urheberschaft der Aufzugsarchitektur. Als eines der Spätwerke von Peter Behrens (1868–1940) entstand 1930 in Charlottenburg-Westend ein zweiflügeliges Mehrfamilienhaus in Stahlskelettbauweise mit Mauerwerksausfachung als vier- bis fünfgeschossige Blockrandbebauung (Abb. 68).[38] Die Hausecke wird akzentuiert durch einen Runderker, der seine Entsprechung an der Hofseite in dem halbrund hervortretenden Treppenhaus findet. Dieses ist sowohl im Wand- als auch im Deckenbereich großflächig matt verglast. In den Aufzugsschacht im Treppenauge sind hohe, mit Maschendraht gesicherte Lichtschächte eingelassen, so daß die Kabine neben Kunst- auch Tageslicht erhält (Abb. 66 und 67). Die Tatsache, daß Treppenhaus und Aufzugschacht formal die Architektur des Gebäudes aufnehmen, unterstützt die Vermutung, daß Peter Behrens für den Gesamtentwurf verantwortlich zeichnete.

Anders verhält es sich bei dem sechsgeschossigen Appartementhaus, das 1929–1930 nach Plänen des Architekten Hans Scharoun (1893–1972) in Wilmersdorf am Hohenzollerndamm gebaut wurde (Abb. 65).[39] Konzipiert als »Junggesellenhaus«, enthält es – ebenso wie das kurz zuvor fertiggestellte Appartementhaus am Kaiserdamm[40] – Einzimmer- und Zweizimmer-Appartements, deren Größe am Hohenzollerndamm zwischen 35 m² und 75 m² differiert. »Die Hauszeile«, so die Beschreibung des Architekten, »besteht [...] aus zwei parallel zueinanderliegenden und durch die Lichthöfe und Treppenanlagen getrennten Zeilen, deren Geschoßhöhen um ein halbes Stockwerk gegeneinander versetzt sind. Obwohl in jedem Stockwerk sechs Wohnungen auf die Treppe münden, wird infolge des Höhenunterschiedes der Eindruck des Mietskasernenhaften vermieden."[41] Insgesamt gibt es vier Treppenhäuser, von denen drei mit Aufzügen ausgestattet sind (Abb. 63). Die Treppenanlagen entsprechen einander in Grundriß und Gestaltung. Charakteristisch für die Zeit ist sowohl die farbige Gestaltung der Treppengeländer mit rotem Handlauf und blauen Sprossen als auch der reduzierte, geometrische Dekor der Schachttüren. Darin spiegelt sich der Einfluß des holländischen *De Stijl* wider – einer Bewegung, die sich 1917 in Leiden um die gleichnamige Zeitschrift für bildende Kunst formierte, welche bis 1931 von Theo van Doesburg (1883–1931) herausgegeben wurde. Die Vertreter von *De Stijl*[42] strebten nach einer elementaren Erneuerung in den Bereichen Architektur, bildende Kunst und Design durch die radikale Reduktion von Form und Farbe. Ihr Ziel war die Abkehr vom Individuellen zugunsten einer objektiv-universalen Gesamtschau mittels einer vollständig vom naturalistischen Vorbild losgelösten Formensprache.[43]

Diese Auffassung steht in deutlichem Gegensatz zur organischen Fassadengestaltung des Appartementhauses am Hohenzollerndamm, dessen auffälligstes Element die dynamische Ecklösung mit halbkreisförmig vorspringenden Balkonen darstellt. Nach J. Christoph Bürkle stammen in beiden Appartementhäusern – sowohl am Kaiserdamm als auch am Hohenzollerndamm – nur die Fassaden von Hans Scharoun.[44] Gegen die Verantwortlichkeit Hans Scharouns für die Gestaltung der Aufzugsschächte spricht überdies eine Anzeige der Firma Schindler aus dem Jahr 1929, die die Aufzüge installierte und mit einer nahezu identischen Anlage für einen »Selbstfahrer«-Aufzug im zeitgemäßen Wohnen« warb. Wenn der Entwurf tatsächlich auf

Schindler-Werbung aus dem Jahre 1929

Schindler advertising from 1929

the influence of the Dutch *De Stijl* – a movement which formed in 1917 in Leiden around the fine arts periodical of the same name which was published until 1931 by Theo van Doesburg (1883–1931). The proponents of *De Stijl*[42] strove for an elementary renewal of the areas of architecture, fine arts and design by a radical reduction of form and colour. Their aim was to turn away from the individual details in favour of an objective and universal overall view with the aid of a formal language that is completely removed from the naturalistic model.[43]

This view is in clear contrast to the organic facade design of the apartment building on Hohenzollerndamm, the most striking element of which is the dynamic corner design and projecting, semi-circular balconies. According to J. Christoph Bürkle, in both apartment buildings – both on Kaiserdamm and on Hohenzollerndamm – only the facades were by Hans Scharoun.[44] A further argument against the responsibility of Hans Scharoun for the design of the lift shafts is an advertisement of 1929 by the Schindler company which installed the lifts and advertised an almost identical lift as a "self-controlled lift for modern living". If the design had really originated from Hans Scharoun, the Schindler company would probably have mentioned him by name – not least because of the fame associated with his name. Probably the lifts were a company design in the contemporary style.

The highlights in the design of lift architecture between the two World Wars also included the cylindrical, glazed shaft in the five storey building of the Nordstern life insurance company which was built in 1935/36 on the steel frame principle to plans by Otto Firle (1889–1966) on Fehrbelliner Platz in Wilmersdorf (Fig. 70). It was the second cylindrical shaft in a building by this architect, who had previously been responsible for the reconstruction of the millinery store of F.V. Grünfeld on Kurfüstendamm, which was demolished in 1969: "The few remaining illustrations of the former store usually show the lift as a special attraction. The shaft surround of glass and nickel-plated bronze rises spirally into the upper storey; the staircase follows the elegant and dynamic upwards flow."[45] The Hungarian artist Laszlo Moholy-Nagy (1895–1947) characterised the dissolution of the static sense of space by reference to the lift shaft in the Grünfeld store: "The boundaries become fluid [...] from the depths to the heights."[46]

An unusual feature on Fehrbelliner Platz is the separation of the lift from the staircase, a means by which the architect suggested an exclusivity

Ein zylindrischer gläserner Schacht mit spiralförmiger Treppe aus dem Jahr 1928 im Wäschekaufhaus Grünfeld von Otto Firle

A cylindrical glass shaft with spiral staircase from 1928 in the F.V. Grünfeld linen store by Otto Firle

Hans Scharoun zurückginge, wäre anzunehmen, daß Schindler diesen namentlich genannt hätte – nicht zuletzt aus Gründen des Renommees, der sich mit dem Namen Scharoun verbindet. Vermutlich handelt es sich eher um einen Firmenentwurf in zeitgemäßem Stil.

Zu den gestalterischen Höhepunkten der Aufzugsarchitektur zwischen den beiden Weltkriegen gehört der zylindrische, gläserne Schacht in dem fünfgeschossigen Gebäude der Nordstern-Lebensversicherung, das 1935/36 in Stahlbetonskelettbauweise nach Plänen von Otto Firle (1889–1966) in Wilmersdorf am Fehrbelliner Platz realisiert wurde (Abb. 70). Es war bereits der zweite zylindrische Schacht in einem Gebäude dieses Architekten, der acht Jahre zuvor für den Umbau des 1969 abgerissenen Wäschekaufhauses F.V. Grünfeld am Kurfürstendamm verantwortlich zeichnete: »Die wenigen heute erhaltenen Abbildungen des ehemaligen Kaufhauses zeigen meist den Aufzug als besondere Attraktion. Die Umwehrung aus Glas und vernickelter Bronze schraubt sich spiralförmig ins Obergeschoß; die Treppe folgt dem elegant-bewegten Aufwärtsschwung.«[45] Der ungarische Künstler Laszlo Moholy-Nagy (1895–1947) charakterisiert die Auflösung des statischen Raumgefühls am Beispiel des Aufzugsschachtes im Kaufhaus Grünfeld: »die grenzen werden flüssig [...] von der tiefe in die höhe«.[46]

Außergewöhnlich ist am Fehrbelliner Platz die Separierung von Aufzug und Treppenhaus, mit der der

Architekt eine Ausschließlichkeit des Weges suggerierte – ein Eindruck, der durch die nachträglichen Türdurchbrüche in der Rückwand des Foyers und den damit auf das Treppenhaus freigegebenen Blick leider verlorenging. Stilistisch kontrastieren hier die schweren Materialien der horizontal gegliederten Architektur des Gebäudes mit der vertikalen Liftstruktur in Glas und Metall, deren Form und Transparenz in überzeugender Weise Technik und Bewegung visualisieren. Die gegensätzliche Auffassung in der Gestaltung der Gebäude- und Aufzugsarchitektur ist keinesfalls als Ergebnis unterschiedlicher Entwurfskonzeptionen zu werten, sondern vielmehr Ausdruck des ästhetischen Zwiespaltes, in dem sich Architekten wie Otto Firle in den dreißiger Jahren befanden.[47]

Die übrigen Beispiele, die hier den Zeitraum von 1918 bis zum Ende des Zweiten Weltkrieges illustrieren, sind geprägt von schlichter Sachlichkeit. Die Funktionalität dominiert bei den Holzkabinen in Umwehrungen aus Maschendraht (Abb. 62 und 69) ebenso wie bei der einfachen Schachttür aus Metall (Abb. 71), die als einziges Gliederungselement ein kleines, schmales Fenster aufweist. Einer der letzten erhaltenen Aufzüge dieses Zeitabschnittes datiert von 1940 und zeigt ein hohes Holzportal mit durchscheinendem Glas im oberen Abschnitt. Beachtenswert ist bei diesem Objekt die Griffmuschel an der Innenseite der Schachttür mit dem geschwungenen Schriftzug des Firmennamens (Abb. 73).

Abschließend stellt sich noch die Frage, ob die Gestaltungsfreiheit in irgendeiner Weise durch polizeiliche Bestimmungen und Verordnungen eingeschränkt wurde. Der erste Versuch einer einheitlichen Regelung »über die Einrichtung und den Betrieb von Aufzügen« datiert von 1899. Ihm folgten mehrere Abänderungen, ehe im September 1925 der »Deutsche Aufzugsausschuß« aus »Vertretern des Reiches, der Länder, der amtlichen Sachverständigen, der Berufsgenossenschaften und der beteiligten Industriegruppen« gegründet wurde.[48] Dieser legte am 30. Juni 1926 die »Techni-

of the routes – an impression that was unfortunately lost by the subsequent doors in the rear wall of the foyer and the resulting visibility of the staircase. Stylistically, the heavy materials of the horizontally subdivided architecture of the building contrast with the vertical lift structure of glass and metal, the form and transparency of which convincingly visualise the technology and movement. The contrasting approaches in the design of the building and the lift architecture is not to be seen as the result of differing design concepts, rather it lends expression to the aesthetic dilemma in which architects such as Otto Firle found themselves in the 1930s.[47]

The other examples which here illustrate the period from 1918 to the end of the Second World War are characterised by a plain functionality. In the wooden cabins this functionality dominates in the surrounds of wire mesh (Fig. 62 and 69) and the simple shaft door of metal (Fig. 71), which was the only structural element to have a small, narrow window. One of the last lifts preserved from this period dates from 1940 and has a high wooden portal with translucent glass in the upper section. A noteworthy element of this lift is the recessed door handle on the inside of the shaft door with the curved inscription of the company name (Fig. 73).

Finally, it must be asked whether freedom of design was restricted in any way by police regulations and statutes. The first attempt at a uniform regulation "for the establishment and operation of lifts" dates from 1899. It was followed by several revisions before in September 1925 the *Deutscher Aufzugsauschuss* (German lifts committee) made up of "representatives of the German Empire, the regional states, officially appointed experts, industrial indemnity associations and participating industrial groups" was established.[48] On 30th June 1926 this committee presented its "Technical principles for the construction of lifts". However, they did not include any direct regulations on the design of the cabin and surrounds apart from details for the minimum height of the cabin and surround, the strength and thickness of the wire mesh and the type of doors.[49] There were also provisions for labelling, although the implementation left scope for artistic design, as was shown in the previous chapter. Apart from details of the manufacturer, year of manufacture and load capacity, this also concerned warnings such as "Caution! Lift!", which were mandatory from 1913 for goods lifts and eight years later also for passenger lifts. There are also individual instructions which are of interest more for their wording than for their design. This applies, for example, to a sign of the Technical Control Board of Berlin with a handwritten date of 24th February 1941:

"CAUTION!
1. Only enter the cabin when the light is on!
2. Do not enter the lift backwards!"[50]

In May of the following year, the "Manufacturing prohibition for all machine construction products and lifts not important for war" was imposed: "Any superfluous advertising to obtain orders for all types of lifts must be refrained from."[51]

The only exceptions were passenger and goods lifts and goods lifts for branches of industry relevant to the war.

»Vorsicht! Aufzug!« – über fünfzig Jahre Kennzeichnungspflicht

"Warning! Lift" – a compulsory warning notice for over fifty years

schen Grundsätze für den Bau von Aufzügen« vor. Sie enthalten jedoch keine unmittelbaren Vorgaben zur Gestaltung von Kabinen und Umwehrung, abgesehen von den Angaben zur Mindesthöhe von Fahrkorb und Umwehrung, Stärke und Dichte des Drahtgeflechtes und zur Art der Türen.[49] Hinzu kommen Hinweise zur Beschilderung, deren Umsetzung ebenfalls die Möglichkeiten künstlerischer Gestaltung bot, wie bereits im vorangehenden Kapitel gezeigt werden konnte. Es handelt sich hierbei, neben Angaben zu Hersteller, Baujahr und Tragkraft, um Warnungen wie »Vorsicht! Aufzug!«, die ab 1913 für Lastenaufzüge und acht Jahre später auch für Personenaufzüge kennzeichnungspflichtig wurde. Darüber hinaus existieren individuelle Hinweise, die weniger aufgrund ihrer Gestaltung als vielmehr wegen des Wortlautes von Interesse sind. Dies gilt beispielsweise für ein Schild des Technischen Überwachungs-Vereins Berlin e.V. mit handschriftlich vermerktem Datum des 24. Februar 1941:

»ACHTUNG!
1. Kabine nur betreten, wenn Licht brennt!
2. Nicht rückwärts in den Aufzug treten!«[50]

Im Mai des darauffolgenden Jahres erging dann das »Herstellungsverbot für nicht kriegswichtige Maschinenbauerzeugnisse und Aufzüge«: »Jede überflüssige Werbung für Hereinbringung von Aufträgen auf sämtliche Aufzugsarten ist zu unterlassen.«[51] Ausgenommen waren nur Personen- und Lastenaufzüge sowie Lastenaufzüge für die kriegsrelevante Industrie.

Kreuzberg
1926 • Flohr
M. Taut,
F. Hoffmann:
Verwaltungsgebäude
administration building

Gebäudeansicht
view of building

Charlottenburg
1929 • Kühnscherf
H. Böttcher:
Wohnhaus
residential building

Wilmersdorf
1930 • Schindler
H. Scharoun:
Wohnhaus
residential building

63

Kabinenantrittsschwelle
cabin entrance threshold

64

65

Gebäudeansicht
view of building

Charlottenburg
1930 • Flohr
P. Behrens:
Wohnhaus
Blick in das
Treppenhaus mit
lichtdurchlässigem
Aufzugsschacht
*residential building
view into the staircase
with a lift shaft that
admits light*

66

67

Kabine
cabin

68

Gebäudeansicht
view of building

Wilmersdorf
1936 • Stahl
O. Firle:
Verwaltungsgebäude
administration building

Wilmersdorf
1934 • Flohr
Bürogebäude
office building

Wilmersdorf
1938 • Flohr
Verwaltungsgebäude
administration building

Wilmersdorf
1940 • Otis
Verwaltungsgebäude
administration building

72

Griffmuschel
in den Türen
recessed handle
in the doors

73

Standardisierung nach 1945

Laut Pressemitteilung waren im Juni des Jahres 1950 von vormals 8600 wieder 3300 Aufzüge in Betrieb, darunter 2291 in den Westsektoren: »35 von ihnen sind Umlauf-Aufzüge, allgemein als ›Paternoster‹ bekannt, und etwa 650 – vorwiegend in Wohnhäusern – sogenannte ›Selbstfahrer‹, die die Hausbewohner benutzen dürfen, ohne vorher eine Prüfung ablegen zu müssen.«[52] Der Begriff »Selbstfahrer« findet sich 1926 in dem »Normalentwurf der Preußischen Aufzugsverordnung« – in Unterscheidung zu geführten Aufzügen, die nur in Begleitung eines geprüften Aufzugsführers genutzt werden dürfen, sowie Umstell- und Umlaufaufzügen. Unter Umstellaufzügen versteht man jene, »die sowohl mit Führerbegleitung zur Beförderung von Personen und Lasten, als auch ohne Führerbegleitung nur zur Beförderung von Lasten dienen.«[53] Zur Illustrierung eines Personen-Umlaufaufzuges oder auch Paternosters ist hier eine Anlage des Jahres 1963 in einem Druckereigebäude (Abb. 85) gezeigt. Bei diesem kontinuierlichen Beförderungssystem sind zwischen zwei parallel verlaufenden, endlosen Kettenschlaufen, die über vier Rollen (Kettenpolygonräder) geführt werden, die Kabinen eingehängt, die langsam auf der einen Seite aufwärts und auf der anderen abwärts laufen. Die Bezeichnung »Paternoster« geht zurück auf den Vergleich der Endloskette mit der Perlenschnur des katholischen Rosenkranzes, deren Perlen verschiedenen Gebeten entsprechen: die kleineren dem »Ave Maria« und die größeren dem »Vater Unser«.

In England entwickelt, wurde dieser Aufzugstyp dort ab 1876 zunächst für den Transport von Waren und ab den frühen 1880er Jahren auch zur Personenbeförderung genutzt. In Deutschland installierte man den ersten Umlaufaufzug 1885 in Hamburg, eingeführt durch den Großkaufmann Freiherr von Ohlendorf (1836–1928),

Standardisation after 1945

According to a press release of June 1950, 3300 of the pre-war 8600 lifts were still in operation, 2291 of them in the western sectors: "35 of them are continuous lifts, generally known as ›Paternoster‹ lifts, and about 650, mainly in residential buildings, are so-called ›self-operating lifts‹ which the residents of the buildings are permitted to use without taking an examination."[52] The term ›self-operating lift‹ is found in 1926 in the *Normalentwurf der Preußischen Aufzugsverordnung* (Draft Prussian Lift Standards Statute) – by contrast to driven lifts which required an examined lift driver, flexible use lifts and continuous lifts. Flexible use lifts are lifts "which can be used both with a driver to convey persons and loads and without a driver to convey loads only."[53] To illustrate a continuous passenger lift or paternoster, a lift in a printing building dating from 1963 is shown (Fig. 85). In this continuous transportation system, the cabins are suspended between two parallel, continuous chain loops which are passed over four pulleys (chain polygon wheels), and the cabins pass slowly upwards on the one side and slowly downwards on the other side. The term "paternoster" goes back to a comparison with the endless chain of pearls in the Catholic rosary in which the pearls represent various prayers: the smaller pearls representing "Ave Maria" and the large pearls the "Lord's Prayer" (Pater noster = Our Father).

This type of lift was developed in England and was initially used there from 1876 for the transport of goods; from the early 1880s it was also used to convey passengers. The first continuous lift in Germany was installed in 1885 in Hamburg, introduced by the merchant Freiherr von Ohlendorf (1836–1928) who had become acquainted with this modern transport system in England.[54] Only twelve years later, in 1907, the Verein Deutscher Ingenieure (Association of German Engineers – VDI) advocated the general introduction of paternoster lifts "because the normal passenger lifts in which a single cell moves up and down is no longer adequate for modern large-scale transport."[55]

The paternoster was the first standardised passenger lift with fixed dimensions, and it was particularly popular in the first three decades of the 20th century. Alongside highly modern lifts, paternoster lifts were also envisaged for the *Wolkenbügel* (Cloud bow) project of the Russian avant garde artist El Lissinsky (1890–1941) of 1924, which was not actually built.[56]

In 1973, because of an unacceptably high accident rate in Germany, there was a nation-wide prohibition of the construction of new passenger circulation lifts, and this was confirmed in 1980 in the statute on lift installations (§ 26). An exception from this provision (which still applies) was for circulation lifts "to convey people who are employed by the operator of the lift" –

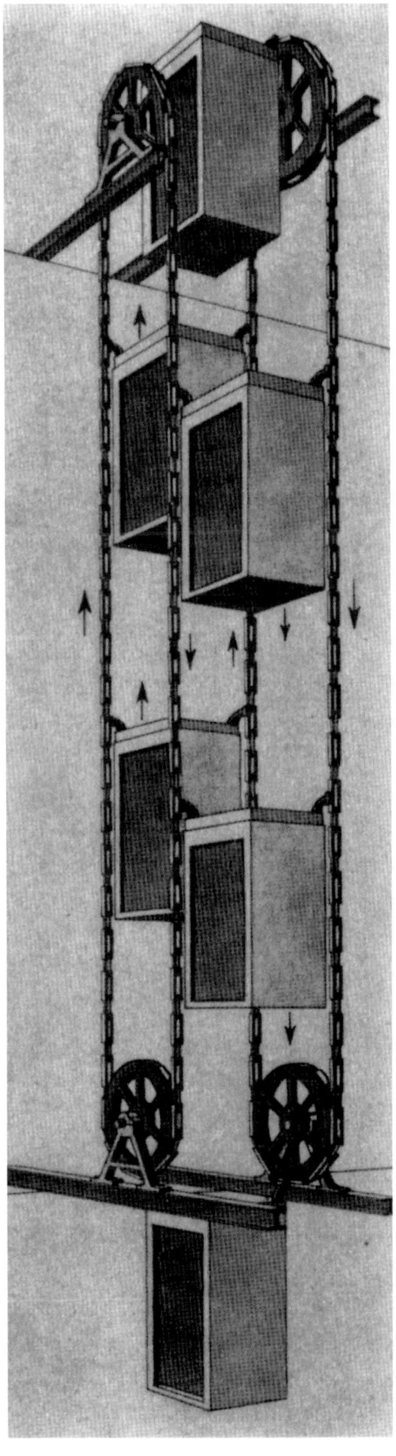

Das Prinzip des Paternosters

The principle of the Paternoster

der dieses moderne Fördersystem in England kennengelernt hatte.[54] Nur zwölf Jahre später, 1907, forderte der Verein Deutscher Ingenieure (VDI) die allgemeine Einführung der Paternosteraufzüge, »da die üblichen Personenaufzüge, bei denen eine einzige Zelle auf- und niedergeht, für großen Verkehr nicht mehr zeitgemäß sind«.[55]

Beim Paternoster handelt es sich um den ersten genormten Personenaufzug mit feststehenden Maßen, der vor allem in den ersten drei Jahrzehnten des 20. Jahrhunderts Konjunktur hatte. Neben modernsten Aufzügen waren Paternoster-Anlagen auch in dem nicht realisierten *Wolkenbügel*-Projekt des russischen Avantgarde-Künstlers El Lissitzky (1890–1941) von 1924 vorgesehen.[56]

1973 erging aufgrund zu hoher Unfallquoten in Deutschland ein bundesweites Verbot zur Neueinrichtung von Personen-Umlaufaufzügen, das 1980 in der *Verordnung über Aufzugsanlagen* (§ 26) bestätigt wurde. Ausgenommen davon waren (und sind) jene Umlaufaufzüge »zur Beförderung von Menschen, die bei dem Betreiber der Anlage beschäftigt sind« – wie in dem hier illustrierten Beispiel von 1963 (Abb. 85).[57]

In den fünfziger Jahren setzte im Aufzugswesen die Standardisierung ein, die eine kostengünstige und schnelle Deckung des steigenden Bedarfs an Neuanlagen zum Ziel hatte. Nachdem in Berlin während des Zweiten Weltkrieges jede dritte Wohnung zerstört worden war, gehörte der Wohnungsbau zunächst zu den vorherrschenden Bauaufgaben.[58] Die steigende Nachfrage an Aufzügen führte bei einigen Unternehmen schon frühzeitig zur Entwicklung von Firmenstandards sowohl für kleinere Bürogebäude als auch vor allem für den Wohnungsbau.[59] Deren vereinheitlichte, kubisch-kompakte Formensprache korrespondiert zwar mit der Rasterbauweise der fünfziger Jahre, zeigt aber nicht die zeittypischen Charakteristika wie die dynamisch-fließende Bewegung, die Verschlankung der Konstruktion und die Materialbelebung.[60] Dem charakteristischen Design jener Zeit begegnen wir heute in nur wenigen Aufzügen, wobei zu bedenken ist, daß eine große Anzahl aus jenen Jahren in der Zwischenzeit schon durch neuere Modelle ersetzt wurde. Zu den erhaltenen Beispielen zählen die dekorativ verkleideten Aufzugstüren einer Anlage des Jahres 1956 mit einer Sonderausführung der Fenster (Abb. 78) ebenso wie ein Entree von 1960 (Abb. 82): Dort wurden die Aufzugstür und die heute ungenutzte Empfangsloge über ovalem Grundriß als Einheit mit breiter Messingrahmung konzipiert. Sowohl Aufzugs- als auch Logentür sind großflächig verglast und unterscheiden sich dadurch unter anderem deutlich von den Türen einer hölzernen Schachtvorderwand, deren Schauöffnungen in Minimalgröße unmittelbar neben den Türgriffen plaziert sind (Abb. 81).

Typisch für jene Zeit ist die Aufzugsgruppe im Gebäude der Hamburg-Mannheimer Versicherung aus dem Jahr 1956 (Abb. 75 und 76). Die Architekten Hans Geber und Otto Risse entwarfen einen dreifach abgetreppten Baukomplex, dessen zehngeschossiger Kopfbau über konkavem Grundriß eine Fassadenverkleidung aus römischem Travertin aufweist, die im Inneren des Hauses an den Wänden des Treppenhauses aufgenommen wird. Die Kabinen hinter den Drehtüren waren ursprünglich – wie zu jener Zeit erlaubt und üblich – ohne Abschlüsse, die hier erst nachträglich eingebaut worden sind.

Die Firmen Flohr Otis und Schindler haben mit ihren frühen standardisierten Personenaufzügen das Marktgeschehen zukunftsweisend beeinflußt und wurden zu Wegbereitern der nationalen und europäischen Normung. Diese entsteht im Deutschen Institut für Normung e.V., »dem runden Tisch, an dem sich Hersteller, Handel, Verbraucher, Handwerk, Dienstleistungsunternehmen, Wissenschaft, technische Überwachung, Staat, d.h. jedermann, der ein Interesse an der Nor-

as in the example from 1963 illustrated here (Fig. 85).[57]

Lift standardisation began in the 1950s and aimed to meet the increasing demand for new lifts more economically and quickly. As every third dwelling in Berlin had been destroyed during the Second World War, residential building was initially one of the major construction tasks.[58] For some manufacturers, the rising demand for lifts led early on to the development of internal company standards both for small office buildings and, in particular, for residential buildings.[59] Their simplified, cubic and compact formal language corresponded with the modular frame building style of the 1950s, but it ignored typical contemporary characteristics such as dynamic flowing movements, slim design and enlivenment of the material.[60] Today, we only encounter the characteristic design of the period in very few lifts; a large number of lifts from that period have since been replaced by more recent models. The examples that are still preserved include the decoratively clad lift doors of a lift from 1956 with a special version of the windows (Fig. 78) and an entrance of 1960 (Fig. 82). In the latter case, the lift door and the reception area that is now unused were designed on an oval floor plan as a unit with a wide brass frame. Both the lift door and the door of the lodge have large glass areas, and this, along with other features, clearly marks them off from the doors of a wooden front wall of the shaft, which has tiny windows openings directly next to the door handles (Fig. 81).

Typical of the period is the lift group in the building of the Hamburg-Mannheimer insurance company dating from 1956 (Fig. 75 and 76). The architects Hans Geber and Otto Risse designed a building complex with three different roof levels. Its ten-storey end block on a concave floor plan has a facade cladding of Roman travertine, and this is taken up again inside the building on the walls of the staircase. The cabins behind the swing doors were originally without car doors, which was permissible at the time – they were only fitted subsequently.

The companies of Flohr Otis and Schindler, with their early standardised passenger lifts, dominated the activities of the market and set the trends, and they paved the way for national and European standardisation. Standards are defined by the "Deutsches Institut für Normung e.V." (German Standardisation Institute, DIN), "the round table at which manufacturers, retailers, consumers, craft companies, service companies, scientists, technical control authorities, the state – i.e. anyone with an interest in standardisation – meet together to ascertain the state of the art and current knowledge and to fix them in writing in German standards."[61] Early standardisation for lifts dating from the 1920s is reflected in three DIN standards sheets from 1926, 1927 and 1929. Among other details, they contain standard dimensions for the continuous passenger lift.[62]

The first post-war meetings on standards for lifts were held in the 1950s. They were attended by representatives of various lift companies (including companies from the GDR), suppliers and industrial companies, members of the Technical Control Board and representatives of the "Deutscher Normenausschuss" (German Standardisation Committee, DNA) and the "Verband deutscher Maschinen- und Anlagenbau e.V." (Association of German Machinery and Plant Manufacturers, VDMA).[63]

The work on standardisation led to the publication in July 1977 of DIN 15306 – a dimensional standard for three types of lift for residential buildings which defines cabin and shaft sizes, carrying capacity, speeds and other dimensions relevant to the building process.[64] In May 1980 there followed DIN 15309 with explanations for lift types in administration buildings and hospitals.[65] This standard covers typical lifts for medium-sized buildings and tall buildings. The cabins have square or transverse rectangular floor plans which, in conjunction with wide doors, enable the passengers to enter and leave the lift quickly (Fig. 131). But transverse rectangular floor plans for cabins also occurred before 1980 (Fig. 83, 92, 95, 100). In Germany

mung hat, zusammensetzen, um den Stand der Technik zu ermitteln und unter Berücksichtigung neuer Erkenntnisse in Deutschen Normen niederzuschreiben.«[61] Von den frühen Normungsarbeiten im Aufzugswesen, die aus den zwanziger Jahren datieren, zeugen drei DIN-Blätter von 1926, 1927 und 1929. Sie enthalten unter anderem Maßnormen zum Personen-Umlaufaufzug.[62]

Die ersten Sitzungen der Nachkriegszeit zum Thema Normung im Aufzugswesen fanden bereits in den fünfziger Jahren statt. Es beteiligten sich Vertreter verschiedener Aufzugsunternehmen (u.a. aus der DDR), Zulieferfirmen und Industrieunternehmen, Mitglieder des Technischen Überwachungs-Vereines e.V. sowie Repräsentanten des Deutschen Normenausschusses (DNA) und des Verbandes Deutscher Maschinen- und Anlagebau e.V. (VDMA).[63]

Im Juli 1977 führte die Normungsarbeit zur Veröffentlichung der DIN 15306 – einer Maßnorm für drei Aufzugstypen im Wohnungswesen, in der Kabinen- und Schachtabmessungen, Tragkräfte und Geschwindigkeiten sowie andere baurelevante Maßeinheiten ausgewiesen sind.[64] Im Mai 1980 folgte DIN 15309 mit Erläuterungen zu Aufzugstypen für Verwaltungsgebäude und Krankenhäuser.[65] Hierin geht es um typische Anlagen für mittlere Gebäudegrößen und Hochhäuser. Die Kabinen zeigen quadratische oder querrechteckige Grundrisse, die in Verbindung mit breiten Türen ein schnelleres Ein- und Aussteigen ermöglichen (Abb. 131). Querrechteckige Kabinengrundrisse begegnen uns allerdings auch schon vor 1980 (Abb. 83, 92, 95, 100). Heute wird der Aufzugsmarkt in Deutschland im Wohnhausbereich zu etwa 80% und in Büro- und Verwaltungsgebäuden zu etwa 50% mit genormten Aufzügen bzw. genormten Hauptkomponenten abgedeckt.

Zur Illustrierung des Abschnittes »Standardisierung nach 1945« wurden überwiegend Aufzugsanlagen in Büro- und Verwaltungsgebäuden ausgewählt, da im Wohnungsbau vornehmlich normierte Produkte ohne architektonische Besonderheiten verwendet wurden. Auch im Bereich der öffentlichen Gebäude zeigt die

Berliner Aufzugsarchitektur zunächst nur eine geringe Anzahl herausragender Lösungen, da hier – im Vergleich mit anderen großen Städten – bis zu Beginn der achtziger Jahre nur wenige repräsentative Bürohäuser, Hotels und andere öffentliche Gebäude entstanden sind. Je nach der Gebäudegröße und Benutzerzahl wurden – nun anstelle von Paternoster – ein oder mehrere Aufzüge in Gruppen installiert. Bei den hier vorgestellten Beispielen der fünfziger Jahre handelt es sich häufig um Zweiergruppen (Abb. 74, 75, 77, 81), von denen die meisten mit mattiert verglasten Schachtdrehtüren und Fahrtrichtungsanzeigern ausgestattet wurden. Üblicherweise handelte es sich dabei um eine Gruppe von Personenaufzügen – zuweilen wurde aber auch ein Personen- mit einem Lastenaufzug kombiniert (Abb. 80). Aus den sechziger Jahren haben sich sowohl Zweier- als auch Dreiergruppen in standardisierter Größe und Ausführung erhalten – wie in dem Beispiel der 1963 installierten Anlage in einem Kommunalbau des Architekten Fritz Bornemann (Abb. 83). Sie zeigt eine für damalige Verhältnisse fortschrittliche Aufzugsgruppe mit zentralöffnenden Schiebetüren, Standortanzeigern und resopalverkleideten Kabinenwänden.

Häufig siegte im Konflikt zwischen Stil und Standard die unauffällige Lösung. Erst Mitte der sechziger Jahre zeichnete sich ansatzweise eine gegenläufige Tendenz ab mit dem dekorativen Einsatz leuchtender Farben und kontrastierender bzw. reflektierender Materialien (Abb. 86, 87, 88, 89). Zudem wurde Metall mit mattierter oder polierter Oberfläche modern und häufiger zur Verkleidung von Schachttüren oder Portalen verwendet (Abb. 89, 90, 96, 99).

In einem Verwaltungsgebäude, welches 1970–73 nach Plänen von Jan und Rolf Rave in Wilmersdorf errichtet wurde, befinden sich zur Regelung des hohen Verkehrsflusses acht Aufzüge um eine große, verkehrsgerechte Lobby (Abb. 91). Die aus der Anordnung der Aufzüge resultierende, horizontale Ausrichtung wird optisch durch die schweren, kompakten Wandstücke zwischen den zurückgesetzten Schachttüren betont.

today, about 80% of residential lifts and 50% of lifts in office and administration buildings have standardised lifts or standardised major components.

The illustrations for the chapter "Standardisation after 1945" mainly show lifts in office and administration buildings because residential buildings largely have standardised products without any special architectural features. Even in public buildings, Berlin's lift architecture only includes a small number of outstanding solutions because up to the beginning of the 1980s – by comparison with other major cities – only a few distinctive office buildings, hotels and other public buildings were built. Depending on the size of the buildings and the number of visitors, a single lift or a group of lifts were now installed instead of paternosters. In the examples from the 1950s presented here there is often a group of two lifts (Fig. 74, 75, 77, 81), most of which had matt glazed swing doors and direction indicators. Normally they were groups of passenger lifts, but sometimes a passenger lift was combined with a goods lift (Fig. 80). From the 1960s, both groups of two and groups of three lifts have been preserved in standardised sizes and versions, such as the example of the lift installed in 1963 in a communal building designed by the architect Fritz Bornemann (Fig. 83). It shows a group of lifts that was progressive for the period, with centrally opening sliding doors, location indicators and cabin walls lined with Formica.

In the conflict between style and standards, the unobtrusive solution often prevailed. It was only around the middle of the 1960s that a counter-tendency began to develop with the decorative use of bright colours and contrasting or reflecting materials (Fig. 86, 87, 88, 89). In addition, metal with a matt or polished surface became modern and was often used as cladding for shaft doors or portals (Fig. 89, 90, 96, 99).

In an administrative building that was built in Wilmersdorf from 1970 to 1973 to plans by Jan and Rolf Rave, the busy flow of traffic is handled by eight lifts grouped around a large lobby suited for a high traffic volume (Fig. 91). The horizontal orientation that results from the arrangement of the lifts is visually emphasised by the massive, compact wall sections between the recessed shaft doors.

An unusual design example from the period is the door surround of a lift group in a packaging and despatch centre that was built from 1971 to 1975 to plans by Hendel, Haseloff and Hotzel (Fig. 95). Following the function of the building, the coloured design of the shaft door surrounds comprise stylised portrayals of folding boxes.

A further unusual example is the installation of a speed indicator in the cabin of a high performance lift from 1976 (Fig. 100). This visualisation of motion by technical means is also found in the wall design in the lobby. There, two groups of three lifts are opposite each other, and the shaft doors and the protruding walls in between are clad with stainless steel. The reflections in this surface convey an impression of movement (Fig. 99).

Our final example from the 1970s is one of the few panorama lifts that were installed in Berlin by the middle of the decade (Fig. 98). It is located in the same building as the group of six lifts mentioned above, and it also dates from 1976. The lift has no ceiling, and for greater transparency the walls are of glass from top to bottom and the horizontal handrail is made of Plexiglas (Fig. 99), as in the group of six. The top and bottom of the cabin wall is enclosed in a polished stainless steel frame. The shaft framework and stair rail are of the same material, and the framework follows the course of the staircase which spirals around the lift.

One of the characteristics of this lift is the rounded corners, which were a fundamental feature of the design and architecture of the 1970s and were as typical of the period as the use of bright colours. However, a comparison with buildings and lifts from the 1980s and 1990s shows that the forms and colours of the 1970s have not had any lasting effect.

Als gestalterische Besonderheit jener Zeit ist die Türumrandung einer Aufzugsgruppe in einem Verpackungs- und Versandzentrum hervorzuheben, welches 1971–1975 nach Plänen von Hendel, Haseloff und Hotzel entstanden ist (Abb. 95). Orientiert an der Funktion des Bauwerkes zeigen die farbig gestalteten Umrandungen der Schachttüren stilisierte Darstellungen von Faltschachteln.

Ebenfalls ungewöhnlich ist die Installation eines Geschwindigkeitsanzeigers in der Kabine eines Hochleistungsaufzuges des Jahres 1976 (Abb. 100). Die auf diese Weise mit technischen Mitteln sichtbar gemachte Bewegung findet architektonisch ihre Entsprechung in der Wandgestaltung der Lobby. Dort stehen sich jeweils drei Aufzüge gegenüber, deren Schachttüren ebenso wie die dazwischenliegenden, vorspringenden Wandstücke mit Edelstahl verkleidet sind. Durch die Reflektionen der Oberflächen wird Bewegung suggeriert (Abb. 99).

Als letztes sei im Kontext der siebziger Jahre einer der wenigen Panorama-Aufzüge vorgestellt, die bis Mitte jenes Jahrzehnts in Berlin installiert wurden (Abb. 98). Er befindet sich im gleichen Gebäude wie die soeben angesprochene Sechsergruppe und datiert ebenso wie diese aus dem Jahr 1976. Im Sinne größtmöglicher Transparenz sind die Wände der deckenlosen Kabine in ganzer Höhe verglast und der horizontale Handlauf, wie auch bei der Sechsergruppe (Abb. 99), aus Plexiglas gestaltet. Den oberen und unteren Abschluß der Kabinenwände bilden polierte Edelstahlrahmen. Aus diesem Material bestehen auch Schachtgerüst und Treppenlauf, wobei die Rahmung des Gerüstes dem Lauf der Treppe folgt, die um den Aufzug herumgeführt ist.

Zu den Charakteristika dieser Anlage gehören die abgerundeten Ecken, die das Design und die Architektur der siebziger Jahre grundsätzlich prägten und für diese ebenso kennzeichnend wurden wie die Verwendung leuchtender Farben. Ein Vergleich mit Bauten und Aufzügen der achtziger und neunziger Jahre zeigt jedoch, daß sowohl die Formen als auch die Farbgebung der siebziger Jahre ohne Nachfolge geblieben sind.

Schöneberg
1952 • Schindler
Bürohaus
office building

Gebäudeansicht
view of the building

76

Charlottenburg
1956 • Schindler
H. Geber, O. Risse:
Bürogebäude
office building

75

Charlottenburg
1956 • Schindler
Universität
university

Friedrichshain
1957 • Arndt
H. Henselmann:
Wohnhaus
residential building

Charlottenburg
1956 • Tenner
P. Schwebes,
H. Schoszberger:
Bürogebäude
office building

Charlottenburg
1959 • Tenner
Bürogebäude
office building

Charlottenburg
1959 • Flohr-Otis
P. Baumgarten:
Bürogebäude
office building

81

Wilmersdorf
1960 • Tenner
Verwaltungsgebäude
administration building

82

Wedding
1963 • Flohr-Otis
F. Bornemann:
Rathaus
town hall

84

Mitte
1964 • Arndt
Verwaltungsgebäude
administration building

85

Kreuzberg
1963 • Schindler
Druckerei
Personalumlaufaufzug
(Paternoster)
printing office
continious passenger lift

Tiergarten
1964 • Schindler
Verwaltungsgebäude
administration building

Schöneberg
1965 • Haushahn
R. Gutbrod,
H. Schwaderer,
H. Kiess:
Bürohaus
office building

Charlottenburg
1966 • Schindler
B. Hermkes:
Universität
university

Charlottenburg
1967 • Schindler
Bürogebäude
office building

DSL-Bank 3
SID 3
kicker 3
Clestra Hauserman 2
DIE ZEIT 4
VOLVO 4
INFRA 4
Clubraum 4
U E 1 2 3 4

Tiergarten
1968 • Flohr-Otis
Bürogebäude
office building

Wilmersdorf
1971 • Flohr-Otis
J. und R. Rave:
Verwaltungsgebäude
administration building

91

Aufzugslobby
lift lobby

92

Wilmersdorf
1971 • Haushahn
Verwaltungsgebäude
administration building

93

Wedding
1971 • Flohr-Otis
Fachhochschule
technical collage

94

Wedding
1972 • Schindler
K. Hendel,
H. Haseloff,
W. Hotzel:
Logistikzentrum
logistics centre

Friedrichshain
1975 • PGH Merkur
Bürogebäude
office building

Mitte
1975 • VEB Sächsischer
Brücken- und Stahlhochbau
H. Graffunder, K.-E. Swora
Veranstaltungszentrum
meeting room

Aufzugsnotruf

Panorama-Aufzug
panorama lift

Wilmersdorf
1976 • Schindler
H. Schäfers,
H.J. Löffler:
Verwaltungsgebäude
administration building

98

Aufzugslobby
lift lobby

99

m/s
U 1 E 1 2 4 5 6 7 8 9 10 11 13 14 15 16 17 18 19 20 22

Charlottenburg
1978 • Schindler
R. Schüler,
U. Schüler-Witte:
Kongreßzentrum
congress hall

101

Außenruftableau
external call panel

102

Kreuzberg
1981 • Schindler
Verwaltungsgebäude
administration building

Die Gegenwart zwischen Tradition und Transparenz

Termini wie Postmoderne, Spätmoderne, Dekonstruktivismus und Neue Einfachheit vermögen vielleicht die architektonische Entwicklung der vergangenen zwei Jahrzehnte zu beschreiben. Sie eignen sich jedoch nur bedingt zur Charakterisierung der Aufzugsarchitektur, da diese in den achtziger und neunziger Jahren eine weitgehend eigenständige Formensprache entwickelt hat.

Nach den Jahren der Standardisierung zeichnet sich in der ersten Hälfte der achtziger Jahre in Berlin erneut eine Wende in der Aufzugsgestaltung ab, die in erster Linie als Belebung durch die Verwendung vielfältiger Materialien zu charakterisieren ist. Den Auftakt hierzu bilden die Aufzugsgruppen im Eingangsfoyer der Grundkreditbank (Abb. 104). Die Anlage besteht aus zwei Zweiergruppen, zusammengefaßt unter einer einfach profilierten Rechteckrahmung aus polychromem Marmor mit schmalen polierten Messingleisten. Zu den dominierenden Materialien zählt hier das glänzende Messing. Es begegnet uns nicht nur im Bereich der Aufzüge, sondern auch an den davor plazierten Fahrtreppen, deren Seitenwände sich in den geschlossenen Schachttüren widerspiegeln.

Das Gebäude der Grundkreditbank wurde 1983–1985 nach Entwürfen von Hans Joachim Pysall, Peter Otto Stahrenberg & Partner errichtet und fällt zeitlich in die Jahre der sogenannten Postmoderne. Angeregt durch die Publikation *The Language of Postmodern Architecture* von Charles Jencks hat sich die Postmoderne in der Architekturdebatte begrifflich etwa Mitte der siebziger Jahre durchgesetzt.[66] Im Unterschied zu Jencks, der einen radikalen Eklektizismus forderte, verband sich für den Kunsthistoriker Heinrich Klotz mit Postmoderne

The Present between Tradition and Transparency

Terms such as Post-Modernism, Late Modernism, Deconstructivism and New Simplicity may possibly describe the architectural development of the last two decades. But they are only partly suitable as a characterisation of lift architecture, which has largely developed its own independent form language during the 1980s and 1990s.

After the years of standardisation, a change in lift architecture began to surface in the first half of the 1980s in Berlin. It can best be characterised as a revival that resulted from the use of a wide range of materials. The first example is provided by the groups of lifts in the entrance foyer of the Grundkreditbank (Fig. 104). There are two groups of two lifts, and each group is joined under a simple profile rectangular frame of polychrome marble, accentuated by slender polished brass. As one of the predominating materials, it can also be found in front of the lifts on the escalators, the sides of which are reflected in the closed shaft doors.

The building was built from 1983 to 1985 to plans by Hans Joachim Pysall, Peter Otto Stahrenberg & Partner, and it thus falls into the period of so-called Post-Modernism. Stimulated by the publication »The Language of Postmodern Architecture« by Charles Jencks, the concept of Post-Modernism established itself in the architectural debate around the middle of the 1970s. [66] By contrast with Jencks, who demanded a radical Eclecticism, the art historian Heinrich Klotz associated Post-Modernism not only with function, but also, and more specifically, with the aspect of the »aesthetic fiction”.[67]

The most prominent example of Post-Modernist architecture in Berlin is the Wissenschaftszentrum (Science Centre) which was built from 1984 to 1987 near the Neue Nationalgalerie to plans by James Stirling. By contrast with the striking facade design, however, the design of the lifts is extremely simple, and thus completely different from the lift architecture in the Stuttgart Staatsgalerie completed in 1984, in which Stirling designed the lift and the shaft framework as a high-tech product in bright colours.[68]

In many lifts from the 1980s and 1990s the dominant material is natural stone in combination with stainless steel and large mirrors. This is illustrated in a 1993 lift in the Art Deco style (Fig. 112) which is concealed behind a Neo-Renaissance building facade. The richness of the material is expressed in the use of red and black granite in the subdivided lift portal and floor of the lift, combined with polished brass in the profile door frame, the matt brass surface of the shaft and cabin door and the suspended cabin ceiling. The interior side walls of the cabins are lined on both sides with dark grey panels, and the rear interior wall consists of a large mirror. The elements that embody the Art Deco style also include the lights in the lobby, which are reflected in the polished surface of the structured granite portal.

We also find effective combinations of heterogeneous materials in two groups of lifts dating from 1994 and 1996 (Fig. 120 and 121): in

Die heute übliche Beschriftung

The usual labeling of today

neben der Funktion vor allem der Aspekt der »ästhetischen Fiktion«.[67]

Prominentestes Beispiel postmoderner Architektur in Berlin ist das Wissenschaftszentrum, das 1984–1987 nach Plänen von James Stirling nahe der Neuen Nationalgalerie erbaut wurde. Im Gegensatz zur auffälligen Fassadengestaltung ist jedoch das Design der Aufzüge äußerst schlicht und unterscheidet sich damit gänzlich von der Aufzugsarchitektur in der 1984 fertiggestellten Stuttgarter Staatsgalerie, bei der Stirling Aufzug und Schachtgerüst als High-Tech-Produkt in leuchtenden Farben konzipierte.[68]

In vielen Aufzügen der achtziger und neunziger Jahren dominiert als Material der Naturstein in Verbindung mit Edelstahl und großflächiger Verspiegelung. Beispielhaft zeigt sich dies in einer Anlage des Jahres 1993 im Stil des Art Déco (Abb. 112), die sich hinter einer Hausfassade der Neorenaissance verbirgt. Der Materialreichtum äußert sich in der Verwendung roten und schwarzen Granits im zweifach abgestuften Aufzugsportal und Fußboden der Lobby, kombiniert mit poliertem Messing in der profilierten Türrahmung und mattiertem Messing zur Verkleidung der Schacht- und Kabinentür sowie in der abgehängten Kabinendecke. Die Innenwände der Kabinen sind beidseitig mit dunkelgrauen Paneelen belegt und rückwärtig großflächig verspiegelt. Zu den Elementen, die den Stil des Art Déco rezipieren, gehören auch die Beleuchtungskörper der Lobby, die sich in der polierten Oberfläche des abgestuften Granitportals widerspiegeln.

Wirkungsvolle Kombinationen heterogener Materialien begegnen uns darüber hinaus unter anderem in zwei Aufzugsgruppen der Jahre 1994 und 1996 (Abb. 120 und 121): im Quartier 206 der Friedrichstadt-Passagen, 1992–1996 erbaut nach Plänen von Pei, Cobb, Freed & Partner, sowie im JannowitzCenter, für dessen 1993–1997 ausgeführten, leicht dekonstruktivistischen Entwurf das Büro Hentrich-Petschnigg & Partner verantwortlich zeichnet. Im Quartier 206 orientiert sich die Gestaltung der Aufzugsanlagen in der

Komposition und der Materialwahl, bei der es sich um eine Kombination aus Marmor und bruniertem Messing handelt, an der Innenarchitektur der Lobby (Abb. 120). Als Besonderheiten sind die trichterförmig erweiterten Laibungen aus Marmor hervorzuheben, die der Aufzugsanlage einen imposanten Charakter geben.

In der hier abgebildeten Dreiergruppe des JannowitzCenters dominiert der Edelstahl in unterschiedlichen Oberflächenbehandlungen (Abb. 121). Die Türen, Türsturze und Ruftableaus zeigen ein dichtes, horizontales Linienraster aus polierten und mattierten Edelstahlflächen, während die seitlichen, horizontal profilierten Kabinenwände das gleiche Material in gebürsteter Form aufweisen. In den Fußböden verbindet sich der Edelstahl – in Gestalt großflächiger Kreisformen – mit einem hellen Naturstein. Die Beleuchtung der Kabinen erfolgt, wie in vielen Anlagen heutiger Zeit, durch sogenannte Downlights, die in die abgehängten Decken aus Milchglas eingelassen wurden und deren Licht von den ganzflächig verspiegelten Rückwänden reflektiert wird.

Als gestalterische Besonderheit ist in diesem Zusammenhang eine Vierergruppe des Jahres 1996 hervorzuheben – und zwar aufgrund der ausgereiften Komposition von farblich und stofflich kontrastierenden Materialien, der qualitätvollen, sorgfältigen Ausführung und einer effektvollen Lichtregie. Der Entwurf stammt – ebenso wie jener der Grundkreditbank – von dem Architekturbüro Hans Joachim Pysall, Peter Otto Stahrenberg & Partner (Abb. 124 und 125). Kontrastreich kombinierte man den dunklen Naturstein Tauerngrün zur Verkleidung der Schachtvorderwand mit hellem Edelholz und hellen Steinfliesen an den Kabinenwänden und -böden. Zur horizontalen Gliederung der Wandflächen wurden polierte Edelstahlleisten eingesetzt, die mit den schmalen polierten Edelstahlbändern auf den mattierten Schachttüren korrespondieren. Zu beachten ist in dieser Anlage vor allem auch die Lichtführung, die den Hell-Dunkel-Kontrast der Materialien wirkungsvoll unterstreicht.

Quartier 206, which forms part of the Friedrichstadt-Passagen and was built in 1992–1996 to plans by Pei, Cobb, Freed & Partner, and in the JannowitzCenter, built in 1993–1997 to a slightly deconstructivist design by Hentrich-Petschnigg & Partner. In Quartier 206, the composition of the lift design and the choice of materials – a combination of marble and burnished bronze – are based on the interior design of the lobby (Fig. 120). The marble door framing, which gives the lift complex an imposing character, is worth noticing.

In the group of three lifts in the Jannowitz-Center that is illustrated here, stainless steel dominates in different surface treatments (Fig. 121). The doors, lintels and call panels show a dense, horizontal line pattern consisting of polished and matt stainless steel surfaces, and the side walls of the cabins have a horizontal profile of the same material in a brushed form. In the floors the stainless steel – in the form of large circular shapes – is combined with a light-coloured natural stone. As in many modern lifts, the cabins are lit by so-called downlights which are set into the suspended frosted glass ceilings and reflected by the rear wall, which consists of a floor to ceiling mirror.

A special example of this type of design is a group of four lifts dating from 1996 – special because of the sophisticated composition of materials contrasting in colour and texture, the high quality, painstaking craftsmanship and an effective use of light. The design – like that of the Grundkreditbank – comes from the architectural office of Hans Joachim Pysall, Peter Otto Stahrenberg & Partner (Fig. 124 and 125). The lifts have a contrasting combination of the dark-coloured "Tauerngrün" natural stone which is used as facing for the front wall of the shaft and the light-coloured precious wood and stone tiles on the cabin walls and floors. The wall surfaces are structured horizontally by polished stainless steel rails, which correspond with the narrow polished stainless steel bands on the matt-coloured shaft doors. The lighting of this lift complex is worthy of special note because it effectively underlines the contrast between the light and dark colours of the materials.

We will now consider some architects who have succeeded in combining the architecture of buildings and lifts in Berlin in a coherent design. This particularly applies to Helmut Jahn (*1940), Oswald Mathias Ungers (* 1926) and Renzo Piano (* 1937), and for the Atrium building in Friedrichstrasse it also applies to the architectural group of von Gerkan, Marg & Partner.

Helmut Jahn, the architect of the Sony-Center that is at present being built on Potsdamer Platz, also designed two previous office buildings in the city which were completed on Kurfürstendamm in 1994 and 1996: »Ku' 70« (Fig. 116) and »Ku' 119« (Fig. 129–131). »Kurfürstendamm 70 [...],« the architect himself states, »is the smallest office building that we have designed so far. It is a gable end building which repairs the sins of urban planning from the 1950s, a knife-like glass structure which at its end becomes a large, visible advertising surface, and is surely one of our most interesting and original buildings.«[69] The eastern facade is subdivided into a large-format, orthogonal grid, which is reflected on a smaller scale on the screen-printed glass surfaces and the walls of the lobby. In view of the narrow width of the plot, Jahn designed the lift as a retracted extension of the narrow, high lobby. Two years later, in 1996, the office building »Ku' 119« was completed at Halensee. Its lobby and lifts represent a highlight of modern lift design in view of the uniform overall composition, the consistent use of high quality materials and the meticulous processing and finish of these materials (Fig. 129–131). The height of the lift access rooms, lift entrance doors and cabins must be noted as a special characteristic.

»Reporting on the architecture of Oswald Mathias Ungers without speaking of the square is like commenting on a work by Günter Uecker without mentioning the word ›nail‹.«[70] This rather flippant comment by the architectural critic Falk Jaeger can also be applied to the design of lifts, such as those in Quartier 205 in the

Im folgenden richtet sich der Blick auf einige Architekten, denen es in dieser Stadt gelungen ist, Gebäude- und Aufzugsarchitektur als gestalterische Einheit zu konzipieren. Dies gilt vor allem für Helmut Jahn (*1940), Oswald Mathias Ungers (*1926) und Renzo Piano (*1937) sowie im Hinblick auf das Atrium-Haus in der Friedrichstraße auch für die Architektengemeinschaft von Gerkan, Marg & Partner.

Von Helmut Jahn, nach dessen Entwürfen in Berlin derzeitig u.a. das Sony-Center am Potsdamer Platz realisiert wird, existieren bereits zwei Bürohäuser in dieser Stadt, die 1994 und 1996 am Kurfürstendamm errichtet wurden: »Ku' 70« (Abb. 116) und »Ku' 119« (Abb. 129–131). »Kurfürstendamm 70 [...]«, so der Architekt selbst, »ist das kleinste Bürohaus, das wir bisher entworfen haben. Es ist eine Giebelbebauung, die die Sünden der Stadtplanung der fünfziger Jahre repariert, ein Messer aus Glas, das am Ende zu einer großen, sichtbaren Werbefläche wird, sicher eines unserer interessantesten und originellsten Gebäude.«[69] Die Ostfassade gliedert sich in ein großformatiges orthogonales Raster, das in kleinerem Maßstab auf die serigraphisch bedruckten Glasflächen sowie die Wände der Lobby übertragen wurde. Der geringen Grundstücksbreite Rechnung tragend, konzipierte Jahn den Aufzug als eine beidseitig eingezogene Verlängerung der schmalen, hohen Lobby. Zwei Jahre später, 1996, wurde das Bürohaus »Ku' 119« am Halensee fertiggestellt, dessen Lobby und Aufzugsanlagen hinsichtlich der einheitlichen Gesamtkomposition, der Verwendung ausschließlich qualitätvoller Materialien und deren sorgfältiger Verarbeitung einen Höhepunkt der heutigen Aufzugsgestaltung darstellen (Abb. 129–131). Die große Höhe der Aufzugsvorräume, Zugangstüren und Kabinen ist als besonderes Kennzeichen hervorzuheben.

»Über die Architektur von Oswald Mathias Ungers zu berichten, ohne auf das Quadrat zu sprechen zu kommen, ist etwa so, als könne man bei der Rezension einer Arbeit von Günter Uecker ohne eine Erwähnung des Wortes ›Nagel‹ auskommen.«[70] Diese etwas saloppe

Feststellung des Architekturkritikers Falk Jaeger läßt sich auch auf die Gestaltung der Aufzüge übertragen, wie das Beispiel aus dem Quartier 205 in den Friedrichstadt-Passagen zeigt (Abb. 119). Der Macht des Quadrates folgend, konzipierte der Architekt ein bis in die Details sorgsam gearbeitetes, orthogonales Raster aus mattiertem Edelstahl, das an den Wänden mit hellen Steinfliesen und in der Decke mit Quadraten aus poliertem Edelstahl ausgefüllt ist. Auch der Kabinenboden besteht – in Fortführung des Bodenbelags der Aufzugslobby – aus quadratischen Steinfliesen. Ungers äußert über Maß, Zahl und Proportion: »Mit der strengen Formgebung wurde ein Grad höchster Vollendung und Einfachheit angestrebt. Übersetzt in die heutige Architektursprache bedeutet dies die Kunst des Weglassens und der Reduktion. [...] Die ideale Gestalt, die perfekte Form stehen im Mittelpunkt des Bestrebens und werden genutzt, um die Ordnung der Welt darzustellen.«[71]

Der italienische Architekt Renzo Piano entwarf das 1997 fertiggestellte Debis-Haus am Potsdamer Platz, dessen großflächige Terrakottaverkleidung des Außenbaues auch im Innern den Wänden des Atriums vorgeblendet ist. Zwei der Aufzugsschächte sind in ganzer Höhe mit horizontalen Terrakottastreben verkleidet, durch deren Zwischenräume der Blick aus den einseitig verglasten Kabinen auf das Atrium freigegeben ist (Abb. 140). Stilistisch entspricht Renzo Pianos Gebäude- und Aufzugsarchitektur der von Vittorio Magnago Lampugnani postulierten »Neuen Einfachheit«, die neben Einfachheit und Klarheit der Formen die Solidität der Materialien und Präzision der Ausführung »als Ausdruck der Verdichtung von Reichtum« fordert.[72]

»Tradition« und »Transparenz« sind Schlüsselbegriffe der gegenwärtigen Aufzugsarchitektur, mit denen sich bestimmte Gebäudetypen bzw. -funktionen verbinden lassen. Als Repräsentationsformen begegnen uns traditionelle Elemente in den Aufzügen großer Hotels, während transparente Schachtverkleidungen mit ebensolchen Kabinen häufig in Verwaltungsgebäuden mit

Friedrichstadt-Passagen (Fig. 119). Using the principle of square elements, the architect created an orthogonal grid of matt stainless steel that is carefully followed through in all its details, and is filled out on the walls with light-coloured stone tiles and in the ceiling with squares of polished stainless steel. Even the cabin floor – which matches the floor covering in the lift lobby – consists of square stone tiles. Ungers commented on the dimension, number and proportion as follows: »The strict form strives to achieve the maximum degree of perfection and simplicity. Translated into the modern language of architecture, this means the art of omission and reduction. [...] The ideal shape, the perfect form are at the centre of our efforts and are used to portray the order of the world.«[71]

The Italian architect Renzo Piano designed the Debis building on Potsdamer Platz which was completed in 1997. The large format terracotta cladding of the outer walls is also used on the interior walls of the atrium. Two of the lift shafts have horizontal terracotta strut cladding, and the cabins are glazed on one side to give the occupants a clear view of the atrium between the struts (Fig. 140). The style of Renzo Piano's building and lift architecture corresponds to the »new simplicity« postulated by Vittorio Magnago; in addition to the simplicity and clarity of forms, this new simplicity demands solid materials and precision of workmanship »as an expression of the concentration of wealth«.[72]

»Tradition« and »transparency« are key concepts in modern lift architecture which can be used to combine certain building types and functions. We encounter traditional elements as luxury features in the lifts of large hotels, whereas transparent shaft cladding and cabins are often seen in administrative buildings with brightly lit inner courtyards and in department stores.

Recalling the traditions of the destroyed grand hotels Adlon and Esplanade, the Grand Hotel on Friedrichstrasse, which is now the Westin Grand, was built in 1986 as »nostalgia in a chandelier glow«.[73] In the lift architecture, this is also expressed in the basketwork arches of the portals and the semi-circular floor position indicators (Fig. 107) – but these elements are counteracted by the use of smoked glass cabin doors and etched stainless steel on the cabin walls.

The Hotel Four Seasons on Gendarmenmarkt, which was completed in 1996, only uses traditional elements in the interior design by the American architect Frank Nicholson. The lift architecture has profiled round arch portals of marble and oak panelling with an egg and dart frame motif in the cabins (Fig. 133). The cabin floors have polychrome incrustations. The eclectic interior design by Nicholson is in stark contrast to the functional and rational facade design by Josef Paul Kleihues.

The lift design in the Hotel Adlon (Fig. 134 and 135) also does not attempt to create a uniform style. The mechanical floor position indicator above the entrance door has ornaments from geometrical Art Nouveau, whereas the embossed and painted leather covering on the shaft doors is adorned with lush arabesques. Inside the cabin, which is lined with precious natural wood, a Plexiglas handrail on the rear wall is combined with the motif of a stylised wreath of leaves in the frame of the mirror. The architects Patzschke & Klotz regard their design for the Hotel Adlon as the beginning of "a 'new tradition' which aims to lead from the degeneration and reduction of the barren modern style to a richly structured architecture."[75] However, the term "new tradition" is self-contradictory in that the new style – including lift architecture – is justified with a traditional vocabulary of forms.

One of the most popular combinations of materials in contemporary lift architecture is glass and steel. In the Berlin of the 1990s we encounter this combination in the atriums of large administrative and office buildings (Fig. 111, 122, 138, 142), in the department stores Lafayette (Fig. 118) and KaDeWe and in exterior lifts (Fig. 114, 117, 126).

The comparison of the almost futuristic design of a group of two lifts from 1992 (Fig. 111) with a lift reduced to its essential elements in the

lichtdurchfluteten Innenhöfen sowie in Kaufhäusern vorkommen.

Erinnernd an die Traditionen der zerstörten Grand Hotels Adlon und Esplanade entstand 1986 mit dem Grand Hotel in der Friedrichstraße, dem heutigen Westin Grand, eine »Nostalgie im Lüsternglanz«.[73] Diese äußert sich auch in der Aufzugsarchitektur in den korbbogenförmigen Portalabschlüssen und mechanischen Etagenanzeigern in Halbkreisform (Abb. 107) – Elemente, die konterkariert werden durch die Verwendung von Schachttüren aus Rauchglas und geätztem Edelstahl an den Kabinenwänden.

Das 1996 fertiggestellte Hotel Four Seasons am Gendarmenmarkt greift nur in der Innenraumgestaltung des amerikanischen Architekten Frank Nicholson traditionelle Elemente auf. Die Aufzugsarchitektur zeigt profilierte Rundbogenportale aus Marmor und kassettierte Eichenvertäfelungen mit dem Eierstab als Rahmungsmotiv in den Kabinen (Abb. 133). Deren Fußböden weisen polychrome Inkrustationen auf. Die eklektizistische Innenausstattung von Nicholson steht gänzlich im Kontrast zu der sachlich-rationalen Fassadengestaltung von Josef Paul Kleihues.

Auch die Aufzugsgestaltung im Hotel Adlon (Abb. 134 und 135) verzichtet auf einen einheitlichen Stil. Der mechanische Etagenanzeiger über der Zugangstür weist Ornamente des geometrischen Jugendstils auf, während die geprägte und bemalte Lederbespannung der Schachttüren mit üppigem Rankenwerk verziert ist. Im Innern der Kabine, die mit edlem Naturholz verkleidet ist, wurde an der Rückwand ein Handlauf aus Plexiglas mit dem Motiv eines stilisierten Blattkranzes in der Rahmung des Spiegels kombiniert. Die Architekten Patzschke & Klotz verstehen das von ihnen entworfene Hotel Adlon als Auftakt zu »einer ›Neuen Tradition‹, die aus den Verkümmerungen und Reduktionen der kargen Moderne zu einer reich gegliederten Architektur führen soll«.[74] Die Formulierung »Neue Tradition« stellt jedoch insofern einen Widerspruch in sich dar, als der neue Stil – auch in der Aufzugsarchitektur – mit einem traditionellen Formenvokabular begründet wird.

Eine der bevorzugtesten Materialkombinationen heutiger Aufzugsarchitektur bilden Glas und Stahl. Sie begegnet uns im Berlin der neunziger Jahre in den Atrien großer Verwaltungs- und Bürogebäude (Abb. 111, 122, 138, 142), in den Kaufhäusern Lafayette (Abb. 118) und KaDeWe sowie im Bereich der Außenaufzüge (Abb. 114, 117, 126).

Der Vergleich einer fast futuristisch gestalteten Zweiergruppe von 1992 (Abb. 111) mit jener auf das Wesentliche reduzierten Anlage im Atrium-Haus der Architektensozietät von Gerkan, Marg & Partner aus dem Jahr 1997 (Abb. 138) führt eindrucksvoll das Streben der Architekten nach immer größerer Transparenz in der Aufzugsgestaltung vor Augen. In Übereinstimmung mit der großzügigen Verglasung der Außenfassade des Gebäudes konzipierten von Gerkan, Marg & Partner ein konstruktives Gerüst aus Stahl mit einer Kabine, die nicht nur gläserne Wände, sondern auch Decke und Fußboden in mattiertem Glas besitzt, und von einer einstöckigen, transparenten Schachtverkleidung umgeben ist. Die formale und materielle Reduktion entspricht dem Ideal der Architektengemeinschaft, »die Dinge so einfach zu gestalten, daß sie inhaltlich und zeitlich Bestand haben. Formale Zurückhaltung und Materialeinheitlichkeit liegen in diesem Bekenntnis begründet, weil für uns Sinnfälligkeit ein kategorischer Imperativ ist.«[75]

Vergleichbar in Stil und Ausdruckskraft sind die zwei gläsernen Aufzugstürme im großen, glasgedeckten Atrium des Willy-Brandt-Hauses, das 1993–1996 nach Plänen der Architektengemeinschaft Helge Bofinger & Partner in der Wilhelmstraße entstanden ist (Abb. 122 und 123). Im Gegensatz zu von Gerkan, Marg & Partner legen Bofinger & Partner in Übereinstimmung mit dem Bodenbelag des Innenhofes die Aufzugskabine mit Natursteinfliesen aus und lassen sie nach oben hin offen ohne Deckenabschluß, so daß die transparente Wirkung hier nochmals eine Steigerung erfährt.

Atrium-building designed by the architectural society von Gerkan, Marg & Partner of 1997 (Fig. 138) shows impressively the striving of the architects for an ever greater transparency in the design of lifts. In keeping with the generous glazing of the exterior facade of the building, von Gerkan, Marg & Partner designed a structural framework of steel with a cabin that not only has glass walls, but also a ceiling and floor of matt glass, and which is surrounded by a single-storey, transparent shaft facing. The formal and material reduction corresponds to the ideal of the architectural society of »designing things so simply that the content will stand the test of time. The formal restraint and uniformity of material are justified by this claim, because rationality is a categorical imperative for us.«[75]

The two glass lift towers in the large, glass-covered atrium of the Willy-Brandt-Haus built in Wilhelmstrasse from 1993 to 1996 to plans by the architectural society Helge Bofinger & Partner are similar in their style and expressive force. (Fig. 122 and 123). By contrast with von Gerkan, Marg & Partner, Bofinger & Partner designed the floor of the lift cabins with natural stone tiles, in keeping with the floor covering of the inner courtyard, and the lift is open at the top to heighten the transparent effect.

And finally, as one of the most recent examples of modern lift architecture, let us consider the lift in the Ludwig-Erhard-Haus of 1998, designed by Nicholas Grimshaw, a master of British high-tech architecture with a striking sense for organic shapes (Fig. 144 and 145). This sense of shape also characterises the lift cabins, which have curved interiors faced with light-coloured wood and stainless steel, whereas the exterior of the cabins is clad with matt aluminium.

Nicholas Grimshaw knows how to use the available contemporary materials in a quality-conscious fashion in order to »express the technological changes of the late 20th century and implement them in architectural form.«[76]

A summary characterising lift architecture in the 20th century appears to be neither reasonable nor possible. The architecture of this century is characterised by frequent changes of style, and the concentrated development of the centre of Berlin as a business and government city has not yet finished. The completion of a number of building projects – for example by Helmut Jahn and Richard Rogers on Potsdamer Platz, by Frank O. Gehry on Pariser Platz and by von Gerkan, Marg & Partner at the new central station (Lehrter Bahnhof) – still lies ahead. In 1997 there were about 6 million lifts in operation throughout the world, about 40,000 of them in Berlin. This number is constantly increasing, which means that the 21st century offers scope for the design of imaginative and striking lift architecture.

Zuletzt sei als eines der jüngsten Beispiele moderner Aufzugsarchitektur die Anlage im Ludwig-Erhard-Haus aus dem Jahr 1998 vorgestellt, entworfen von Nicholas Grimshaw, einem Meister der britischen High-Tech-Architektur mit ausgeprägtem Sinn für organische Formgebung (Abb. 144 und 145). Letztere kennzeichnet auch die Aufzugskabinen, deren geschwungene Innenräume mit hellem Holz und Edelstahl ausgestattet sind, während die äußere Schale mit mattiertem Aluminium verkleidet ist. Nicholas Grimshaw versteht es, die ihm zugänglichen zeitgenössischen Materialien qualitätsbewußt zu verwenden und mit diesen, »die technologischen Veränderungen des späten 20. Jahrhunderts auszudrücken und architektonisch umzusetzen«.[76]

Eine zusammenfassende Charakterisierung der Aufzugsarchitektur des 20. Jahrhunderts erscheint weder sinnvoll noch möglich: Einerseits ist die Architektur dieses Jahrhunderts von häufig wechselnden Stilrichtungen gekennzeichnet, andererseits die Verdichtung der Mitte Berlins zur Geschäfts- und Regierungsstadt noch nicht abgeschlossen. Die Vollendung einer Vielzahl von Bauwerken – u.a. von Helmut Jahn und Richard Rogers am Potsdamer Platz, Frank O. Gehry am Pariser Platz oder von Gerkan, Marg & Partner am Lehrter Bahnhof – steht noch aus. 1997 waren weltweit ca. 6 Millionen Aufzüge in Betrieb und etwa 40000 davon in Berlin. Die Tendenz ist steigend und bietet somit auch für das 21. Jahrhundert die Möglichkeit zum Entwurf ausgefallener, markanter Aufzugsarchitekturen.

Gebäudeansicht
view of the building

105

Charlottenburg
1984 • Schindler
H. Pysall,
P. Starenberg,
J. Grundei:
Verwaltungsgebäude
administration building

104

Mitte
1985 • VEB Aufzug- und Fahrtreppenbau
Bürogebäude
office building

106

Mitte
1986 • Flohr-Otis
Hotel
hotel

107

Charlottenburg
1987 • Schindler
Hotel
hotel

Charlottenburg
1956 • Flohr-Otis
Bürogebäude
(modernisiert 1991)
office building
(modernised in 1991)

110

Tiergarten
1988 • Haushahn
J. Sawade:
Hotel
hotel

109

111

Tiergarten
1992 • Kone
Bassenge,
Puhan-Schulz,
Heinrich,
Schreiber:
Bürogebäude
office building

Mitte
1993 • Otis
H. Schönberger:
Bürogebäude
office building

Mitte
1993 • Thyssen
Rathaus
town hall

114

Tiergarten
1993 • Sange
P. Träger:
Bürogebäude
Außenaufzug
office building
exterior lift

115

Blick durch die
Panoramakabine
view through the
panorama cabin

Charlottenburg
1994 • Thoma
Murphy / Jahn:
Bürogebäude
Blick in die
Aufzugslobby
und Kabine
office building
view of the lift
lobby and cabin

Mitte
1994 • Lutz
Bürogebäude
office building

Mitte
1994 • Otis
J. Nouvel:
Kaufhaus
department store

Mitte
1994 • Schindler
O.M. Ungers:
Bürogebäude
office building

Mitte
1994 • Otis
Pei, Cobb,
Freed & Partner:
Bürogebäude
office building

120

Mitte
1995 • Otis
HPP Hentrich-
Petschnigg & Partner:
Bürogebäude
office building

121

Kreuzberg
1995 • Vestner
H. Bofinger & Partner:
Verwaltungsgebäude
administration building

Panorama-Kabine
panorama cabin

Mitte
1996 • Schindler
Pysall, Stahrenberg & Partner:
Verwaltungsgebäude
Blick in eine Aufzugskabine
administration building view into a lift cabin

124

Aufzugsgruppe
group of lifts

125

Kreuzberg
1995 • Selzer
I. Horn:
Bürogebäude
office building

Wilmersdorf
1996 • Tepper
H. Léon,
K. Wohlhage:
Bürogebäude
office building

Mitte
1996 • Haushahn
J.P. Kleihues:
Bürogebäude
Blick in die
Aufzugslobby
office building
view of the lift lobby

Wilmersdorf
1996 • Schindler
Murphy / Jahn:
Bürogebäude
Aufzugslobby
office building
lift lobby

Gebäudeansicht
view of the building

129

Aufzugskabine
lift cabin

130

ZUM
TREPPENHAUS Nr.4

Mitte
1996 • Sange
Verwaltungsgebäude
administration building

Mitte
1996 • Otis
F. Nicholson:
Hotel
hotel

Blick in eine
Aufzugskabine
view into a lift cabin

Mitte
1997 • Schindler
Patzschke & Klotz:
Hotel
hotel

-3-2-1E123456

Mitte
1997 • Schindler
von Gerkan,
Marg & Partner:
Bürogebäude
office building

136

Charlottenburg
1997 • Kone
H. Pysall,
P. Starenberg:
Bürogebäude
office building

Tiergarten
1997 • Thyssen
S-Bahnstation
urban railway station

137

Mitte
1997 • Schoppe & Keil
Fremerey:
Bürogebäude
office building

Tiergarten
1997 • Schindler
R. Piano,
Ch. Kohlbecker:
Verwaltungsgebäude
Kabinenansicht
administration building
view of the cabin

140

Aufzugsgruppe
group of lifts

141

Mitte
1997 • Schindler
C. Mäckler:
Bürogebäude
office building

142

Mitte
1997 • Otis
von Gerkan,
Marg & Partner:
Verwaltungsgebäude
administration building

Charlottenburg
1997 • Otis und Schindler
N. Grimshaw & Partner:
Börsen- und Bürogebäude
Außenansicht der Kabine
stock exchange and office building
exterior view of the cabin

Kabine
cabin

Anmerkungen

1. Ausnahmen bilden Abb. 15 und 45 mit Anlagen, die heute außer Betrieb sind.
2. Bruno Bruognolo: »Technische Voraussetzungen für den Bau von Hochhäusern«, in: Ausst.Kat. *Der Schrei nach dem Turmhaus. Der Ideenwettbewerb Hochhaus am Bahnhof Friedrichstraße Berlin 1921/22.* Ausstellung im Bauhaus-Archiv Museum für Gestaltung, Berlin 1988, S. 227.
3. Albert Gessner: *Das deutsche Miethaus – ein Beitrag zur Städtekultur der Gegenwart.* München 1909, S. 2.
4. A. Gessner, wie Anm. 3, S. 128–129.
5. Armin von Gerkan: *Das Theater von Priene als Einzelanlage und in seiner Bedeutung für das hellenistische Bühnenwesen.* München/Berlin/Leipzig 1921, S. 68f.
6. Für die Konstruktion eines Drehkranes sprachen sich aus: Wilhelm Dörpfeld, Emil Reisch: *Das Griechische Theater.* Athen 1896 (Nachdruck 1966), S. 232; Martin Schede: *Die Ruinen von Priene.* Berlin 1964, S. 76. Solche Krananlagen dienten im griechischen Theater dem Transport »schwebender« Theatergötter. Von ihnen leitet sich der lateinische Ausdruck *deus ex machina* (»der Gott aus der Maschine«) ab – für einen unerwarteten Helfer in der Not.
7. Jeannot Simmen, Uwe Drepper: *Der Fahrstuhl – Die Geschichte der vertikalen Eroberung.* München 1984, S. 205.
8. Diese Information verdanken wir dem Deutschen Archäologischen Institut Rom, das seit 1996 in Zusammenarbeit mit der Soprintendenza Archeologica Roma das Untergeschoß des Kolosseums erforscht. Ein erster ausführlicher Bericht über die Aufzugsysteme im Kolosseum erscheint Ende dieses Jahres in den *Römischen Mitteilungen 105* (1998).
9. Eine mögliche Rekonstruktion findet sich bei Benvenuto Frau: *I Polyspastos. Note di technologica meccanica antica.* Rom 1980, S. 56, und bei Simmen/Drepper, wie Anm. 7, S. 206, Abb. 227.
10. Herbert Droege: *Schindler Aufzüge – Leitfaden für Mitarbeiter unserer Montage-Abteilung.* Frankfurt/Main 1971, S. 5; B. Frau, wie Anm. 9, S. 47.
11. Günther Binding (Hg.): *Der mittelalterliche Baubetrieb Westeuropas.* Katalog der zeitgenössischen Darstellungen, Köln 1987, Nachträge Köln 1992; G. Binding: *Baubetrieb im Mittelalter.* Darmstadt 1993, S. 393–426.
12. Ingo F. Walther: *Codex Manesse. Die Miniaturen der Großen Heidelberger Liederhandschrift.* Frankfurt am Main 1988, S. 62–63 und Tafel 31.
13. Dies bestätigt eine Tuschezeichnung in dem Meteora-Kloster Vaarlam: vgl. hierzu Friederike Kyrieleis: *Kunstdenkmäler in Griechenland – Ein Bildhandbuch: Festland.* München/Berlin 1982, Abb. 199.

Notes

1. Exceptions are Fig. 15 and Fig. 45, which show lifts that are not in operation today.
2. Bruno Bruognolo: "Technische Voraussetzungen für den Bau von Hochhäusern" in the catalogue of the exhibition: *Der Schrei nach dem Turmhaus. Der Ideenwettbewerb Hochhaus am Bahnhof Friedrichstraße Berlin 1921/22.* Exhibition in the Bauhaus Archive, Museum of Design, Berlin 1988, p. 227.
3. Albert Gessner: *Das deutsche Miethaus – ein Beitrag zur Städtekultur der Gegenwart.* Munich 1909, p. 2
4. A. Gessner, op. cit., p. 128–129.
5. Armin von Gerkan: *Das Theater von Priene als Einzelanlage und in seiner Bedeutung für das hellenistische Bühnenwesen.* Munich/Berlin/Leipzig 1921, p. 68f.
6. An interpretation of the structure as a rotary crane was advocated by Wilhelm Dörpfeld and Emil Reisch in: *Das Griechische Theater.* Athens 1896 (reprinted 1966), p. 232, and by Martin Schede in *Die Ruinen von Priene.* Berlin 1964, p. 76. In Greek theatre, cranes were used to transport theatrical gods floating on air. This was the origin of the Latin term *deus ex machina* (the god out of the machine) for an unexpected helper in a time of need.
7. Jeannot Simmen, Uwe Drepper: *Der Fahrstuhl – Die Geschichte der vertikalen Eroberung.* Munich 1984, p. 205.
8. This information is provided by the German Archaeological Institute in Rome which has been exploring the lower storey of the Colosseum since 1996 in cooperation with the Soprintendenza Archeologica Roma. A first detailed report on the lift systems in the Colosseum will be published at the end of this year in *Römische Mitteilungen 105* (1998).
9. A possible reconstruction is found in Benvenuto Frau: *I Polyspastos. Note di technologica meccanica antica.* Rome 1980, p. 56; Simmen/Drepper, op. cit., p. 206, Fig. 227.
10. Herbert Droege: *Schindler Aufzüge – Leitfaden für Mitarbeiter unserer Montage-Abteilung.* Frankfurt/Main 1971, p. 5; B. Frau, op. cit., p. 47.
11. Günther Binding (ed.): *Der mittelalterliche Baubetrieb Westeuropas. Katalog der zeitgenössischen Darstellungen.* Cologne 1987, supplements Cologne 1992; G. Binding: *Baubetrieb im Mittelalter.* Darmstadt 1993, p. 393–426.
12. Ingo F. Walther: *Codex Manesse. Die Miniaturen der Großen Heidelberger Liederhandschrift.* Frankfurt/Main 1988, p. 62–63 and plate 31.
13. This is confirmed by an ink drawing in the Meteora monastery of Vaarlam; cf. Friederike Kyrieleis: *Kunstdenkmäler in Griechenland – Ein Bildhandbuch: Festland.* Munich/Berlin 1982, p. 199.
14. Erhard Weigel: *Mathematische Kunstübungen.* Jena 1669, p. 72; cf. also Simmen/Drepper, op. cit., p. 196.

15. Leonhardt Christoph Sturm: *Podromus – Architecturae Goldmanianae.* Augsburg 1714.
16. Quoted from Simmen/Drepper, op. cit., p. 201.
17. Simmen/Drepper, op. cit., Fig. 16.
18. Bruce Brooks Pfeiffer: *Frank Lloyd Wright Drawings – Masterworks from the Frank Lloyd Wright Archives.* New York 1990, p. 117–119.
19. Cf. Wolfgang Schäche: "Baugeschichte und Stadtbild bis 1945", in *Berlin Handbuch – Das Lexikon der Bundeshauptstadt Berlin.* Berlin 1993, p. 210–219.
20. *Berlin und seine Bauten. Teil II, Rechtsgrundlagen und Stadtentwicklung.* Edited by the Architekten- und Ingenieur-Verein zu Berlin. Berlin 1964, p. 41.
21. *Carl Flohr. Maschinenfabrik Berlin. Jubiläumsschrift.* Berlin 1900, p. 14.
22. Carl Flohr, op. cit., p. 43.
23. Leutfried Gradmann: "Neuzeitliche Aufzugsanlagen" in: *Der Bau- und Kunstschlosser. Illustrierte Fachzeitschrift 22.* 1921, p. 505.
24. Adolf Behne: "Bemerkungen zum Thema: Moderne Baukunst", in: Max Taut: *Bauten und Pläne.* Berlin 1927 (reprint 1996 with a postscript by Tilmann Buddensieg, p. 14).
25. Wolfgang Götz: "Historismus – Ein Versuch zur Definition des Begriffes", in: *Zeitschrift des deutschen Vereins für Kunstwissenschaft,* No. 24, 1970, p. 196–212, especially p. 201.
26. Beate Dry von Zezschwitz: "Jugendstil", in: *Jugendstil – Gegenstände aus Bielefelder Privatbesitz,* exhibition catalogue, Bielefelder Kunstverein (Bielefeld art association) 1986, p. 9.
27. The Wiener Werkstätten (Viennese workshops) arose from the Viennese secession of 1897. They were established in 1903 by the architect Josef Hoffmann, the painter Koloman Moser and the banker Fritz Wärndorfer. Hoffmann and Moser became the creators of the geometrical black and white style. From about 1902 their work, similar to the furniture designed by the Scottish architect, designer and painter Charles Rennie Mackintosh, showed a tectonic strictness in its basic geometrical forms. The business premises of the furniture company of Jacob & Josef Kohn were built in Leipziger Strasse in Berlin in 1905–1906 to plans by Hoffmann and Moser. Cf. *Berlin und seine Bauten, Teil VIII, Bauten für Handel und Gewerbe, volume A "Handel".* Edited by the Architekten- und Ingenieur-Verein zu Berlin (Berlin association of architects and engineers), Berlin/Munich/Düsseldorf 1978, p. 182.
29. The photograph shown in the text, today in the AEG-Archive, was taken on 19th January 1907.
29. Cf. Tilmann Buddensieg, Henning Rogge: *Industriekultur – Peter Behrens und die AEG 1907–1914.* Berlin (3rd edition) 1990, p. 41, Fig. 32.
30. Adolf Behne: "Bemerkungen zum Thema: Moderne Baukunst", in: Max Taut: *Bauten und Pläne.* Berlin 1996 (reprint of the edition of 1927), p. 15 and 20–21.

14. Erhard Weigel: *Mathematische Kunstübungen.* Jena 1669, S. 72; siehe auch Simmen/Drepper, wie Anm. 7, S. 196.
15. Leonhardt Christoph Sturm: *Prodromus – Architecturae Goldmanianae.* Augsburg 1 714.
16. zitiert nach Simmen/Drepper, wie Anm. 7, S. 201.
17. Simmen/Drepper, wie Anm. 7, Abb. 16.
18. Bruce Brooks Pfeiffer: *Frank Lloyd Wright Drawings – Masterworks from the Frank Lloyd Wright Archives.* New York 1990, S. 117–119.
19. Vgl. hierzu Wolfgang Schäche: »Baugeschichte und Stadtbild bis 1945«, in: *Berlin Handbuch – Das Lexikon der Bundeshauptstadt.* Berlin 1993, S. 210–219.
20. *Berlin und seine Bauten. Teil II, Rechtsgrundlagen und Stadtentwicklung.* hg. v. Architekten- und Ingenieur-Verein zu Berlin. Berlin 1964, S. 41.
21. *Carl Flohr, Maschinenfabrik Berlin, Jubiläumsschrift.* Berlin 1900, S. 14.
22. Carl Flohr, wie Anm. 21, S. 43.
23. Leutfried Gradmann: »Neuzeitliche Aufzugsanlagen.«, in: *Der Bau- und Kunstschlosser. Illustrierte Fachzeitschrift 22.* 1921, S. 505.
24. Adolf Behne: »Bemerkungen zum Thema: Moderne Baukunst«, in: Max Taut: *Bauten und Pläne.* Berlin 1927 (Reprint 1996 mit einem Nachwort von Tilmann Buddensieg, S. 14).
25. Wolfgang Götz: »Historismus – Ein Versuch zur Definition des Begriffes«, in: *Zeitschrift des deutschen Vereins für Kunstwissenschaft* 24. 1970, S. 196-212, insbes. S. 201.
26. Beate Dry-von Zezschwitz: »Jugendstil«, in: *Jugendstil – Gegenstände aus Bielefelder Privatbesitz.* Ausst.Kat. Bielefelder Kunstverein e.V. 1986, S. 9.
27. Die Wiener Werkstätten gingen aus der 1897 gegründeten Wiener Sezession hervor. Sie wurden 1903 von dem Architekten Josef Hoffmann, dem Maler Koloman Moser und dem Bankier Fritz Wärndorfer ins Leben gerufen. Hoffmann und Moser wurden zu Urhebern des geometrischen Schwarz-Weiß-Stiles. Ab etwa 1902 kennzeichnet ihre Arbeiten, ebenso wie die Möbel des schottischen Architekten, Designers und Malers Charles Rennie Mackintosh, eine tektonische Strenge in den Grundformen der Geometrie. In Berlin entstanden nach den Entwürfen von Hoffmann und Moser 1905–1906 in der Leipziger Straße die Geschäftsräume der Möbelfirma Jacob & Josef Kohn. Vgl. *Berlin und seine Bauten, Teil VIII. Bauten für Handel und Gewerbe. Band A Handel.* Hg. v. Architekten- und Ingenieur-Verein zu Berlin, Berlin/München/Düsseldorf 1978, S. 182.
28. Die im Text abgebildete Fotografie, heute im AEG-Archiv, entstand am 19. Januar 1907.

29. Vgl. Tilmann Buddensieg, Henning Rogge: *Industriekultur – Peter Behrens und die AEG 1907–1914.* Berlin (3. Aufl.) 1990, S. 41, Abb. 32.
30. Adolf Behne: »Einige Bemerkungen zum Thema: Moderne Baukunst«, in: Max Taut: *Bauten und Pläne.* Berlin 1996 (Reprint der Erstausgabe von 1927), S. 15 und 20–21.
31. *Neue Sachlichkeit – Deutsche Malerei seit dem Expressionismus.* Katalog zur Ausstellung der Städtischen Kunsthalle Mannheim, 14. 6.–13.9.1925. Mannheim 1925.
32. Walter Curt Behrendt: *Der Sieg des neuen Baustils.* Stuttgart 1927, zitiert nach: *trotzdem modern – Die wichtigsten Texte zur Architektur in Deutschland.* ausgewählt und kommentiert von Kristiana Hartmann, Braunschweig/Wiesbaden 1994, S. 135.
33. Zitiert nach Simmen/Drepper, wie Anm. 7, S. 90.
34. Zur Architektur des Gebäudes vgl. *Bauwelt* 17, 1926, Heft 31, S. 725–736; Rudolf Bernhard: »Das Haus des Verbandes der deutschen Buchdrucker zu Berlin«, in: *Deutsche Bauzeitschrift (Konstruktion und Ausführung)* 60, 1926, S. 73–79; Max Taut, wie Anm. 30, S. 25–64.
35. Das Gerüst wurde fabriziert von der Berliner Firma Schulz und Holdefleiss.
36. Vgl. Adolf Behne, wie Anm. 30, S. 8.
37. Ursprünglich war das ganze Treppenhaus auf diese Weise verkleidet. Die schwarzen Fliesen an der linken Wand sind eine Zutat der Nachkriegszeit.
38. Vgl. Ernst Heinrich: »Mehrgeschossiger privater Mietshausbau auf Einzelgrundstücken von 1896–1933«, in: *Berlin und seine Bauten, Teil IV Wohnungsbau, Band B, Die Wohngebäude – Mehrfamilienhäuser.* hg.v. Architekten- und Ingenieur-Verein zu Berlin, Berlin/München/Düsseldorf 1974, S. 72, Abb. 93 (Ansicht mit Runderker); Hans-Henning Joeres, Barbara Schulz: »Liste der Mehrfamilienhäuser 1918–1945«, in: ebd., Objekt 936, S. 397 (mit Grundriß).
39. Vgl. *Berlin und seine Bauten IV B*, wie Anm. 38, Objekt 957, S. 31, 71 und S. 415 (mit Grundriß).
40. Vgl. *Berlin und seine Bauten IV B*, wie Anm. 38, Objekt 924, S. 331, Abb. 29, S. 387 (mit Grundriß).
41. Hans Scharoun: »Junggesellenhaus am Hohenzollerndamm in Berlin-Wilmersdorf«, in: *Bauwelt* 23, 1932, H. 6, S. 155.
42. Hierzu zählen neben Theo van Doesburg unter anderem der Maler Piet Mondrian (1872–1944) und die Architekten J. J. P. Oud (1890–1963) und Gerrit Rietveld (1888–1964).
43. Vgl. hierzu »De Stijl – Manifest I vom November 1918«, in: Ulrich Conrads: *Programme und Manifeste zur Architektur des 20. Jahrhunderts.* Frankfurt/M. 1964, S. 36-37 (= *Bauwelt Fundamente 1*).
44. J. Christoph Bürkle: *Hans Scharoun.* Zürich/München/London 1993, S. 74. Für die Appartementhäuser am Kaiser-

31. *Neue Sachlichkeit – Deutsche Malerei seit dem Expressionismus.* Catalogue of an exhibition in the Städtische Kunsthalle Mannheim, 14.6–13.9.1925, Mannheim 1925.
32. Walter Curt Behrendt: "Der Sieg des neuen Baustils", Stuttgart 1927, quoted from: *trotzdem modern – Die wichtigsten Texte zur Architektur in Deutschland.* Selected and commented by Kristiana Hartmann, Braunschweig/Wiesbaden 1994, p. 135.
33. Quoted from Simmen/Drepper, op. cit., p. 90.
34. On the architecture of the building cf. *Bauwelt 17*, 1926, No. 31, p. 725–736; Rudolf Bernhard: "Das Haus des Verbandes der deutschen Buchdrucker zu Berlin" in: *Deutsche Bauzeitschrift (Konstruktion und Ausführung) 60*, 1926, p. 73–79; Max Taut, op. cit., p. 25–64.
35. The frame was made by the Berlin company of Schulz and Holdefleiss.
36. Cf. Adolf Behne, op. cit., p. 8.
37. Originally the whole staircase was tiled in this way. The black tiles on the left wall were added after the War.
38. Cf. Ernst Heinrich: "Mehrgeschossiger privater Mietshausbau auf Einzelgrundstücken von 1896–1933", in: *Berlin und seine Bauten, part IV "Wohnungsbau", volume B "Die Wohngebäude – Mehrfamilienhäuser".* Edited by the Architekten- und Ingenieur-Verein zu Berlin. Berlin/Munich/Düsseldorf 1974, p. 72, Fig. 93 (view with round bay); Hans-Henning Joeres, Barbara Schulz, "Liste der Mehrfamilienhäuser 1918–1945" in: ibid., object 936, p. 397 (with floor plan).
39. Cf. *Berlin and its buildings IV B*, op. cit., object 957, p. 31, 71 and 415 (with floor plan).
40. Cf. *Berlin and its buildings IV B*, op. cit., object 924, p. 331, Fig. 29, p. 387 (with floor plan).
41. Hans Scharoun: "Junggesellenhaus am Hohenzollerndamm in Berlin-Wilmersdorf", in: *Bauwelt 23*, 1932, No. 6, p. 155.
42. Apart from Theo van Doesburg, they also included the painter Piet Mondrian (1872–1944) and the architects J.J.P. Oud (1890–1963) and Gerrit Rietveld (1888–1964).
43. Cf. the "De Stijl manifesto I" of November 1918, in: Ulrich Conrads: *Programme und Manifeste zur Architektur des 20. Jahrhunderts*, Frankfurt/M. 1964, p. 36–37.
44. J. Christoph Bürkle: *Hans Scharoun.* Zürich/Munich/London 1993, p. 74. For the apartment buildings on Kaiserdamm the author adds: "the one and two room flats for households of one to two persons [...] were not planned by Scharoun, but were prescribed by the company and designed by Georg Jacobowitz. Scharoun therefore only designed the facades – an unusual event in his oeuvre [...]" (p. 70). Unfortunately, Bürkle does not name a source.
45. Simmen/Drepper, op. cit., p. 90.
46. Laszlo Moholy-Nagy: *Von Material zu Architektur.* Facsimile of the original edition published in 1929, Mainz/Berlin 1968, p. 222, Fig. 199.

47. Wolfgang Schäche: *Architektur und Städtebau in Berlin zwischen 1933 und 1945 – Planen und Bauen unter der Ägide der Stadtverwaltung.* Berlin 1992, p. 266 –268.
48. H. Jaeger: *Bestimmungen über Einrichtung und Betrieb der Aufzüge.* Berlin 1930, p. 12.
49. Where the police regulations of 30th May 1913 still prescribed a surround height of 1.80 m, this was increased from 1926 to a minimum height of 2.50 m. The height of the cabin had to be at least 1.80 m. Cf. H. Jaeger, op. cit., p. 85 (surround), p. 86 (doors), p. 104 (cabin).
50. The sign is now in the archive of the Gottschalk & Michaelis company.
51. Cf. the circular of the Technical Control Board of Berlin of 17th December 1942 in the archive of the TÜV (Technical Control Board).
52. *Die Welt,* 25th June 1950.
53. H. Jaeger, op. cit., p. 16.
54. Simmen/Drepper, op. cit., p. 223–224.
55. *Zentralblatt der Bauverwaltung,* No. 20, 11th March 1908, p. 147.
56. Cf. El Lissitzky: Proun und Wolkenbügel – Schriften, Briefe, Dokumente. Edited by Sophie Lissitzky-Küppers and Jens Lissitzky, Dresden 1977, 82. El Lissitzky developed the "Cloud bow" project in collaboration with Mart Stam (1899–1986) and Emil Roth.
57. Cf. "Bundesdeutsche Aufzugsverordnung" of 28th March 1972, paragraph 28, in the Federal Gazette; "Verordnung über Aufzugsanlagen (Aufzugsverordnung)", paragraph 26, in: *TRA – Technische Regeln für Aufzüge.* Paperback edition 1992, published by the Verband der Technischen-Überwachungs-Vereine e.V. (Association of Technical Control Boards), Cologne/Berlin 1992, p. 15.
58. *Berlin-Handbuch,* op. cit., p. 1389.
59. In 1954 Otis developed the "SWA" – the standard residential lift for four persons with swng shaft doors and wooden cabins without cabin terminations. In 1955 Schindler produced the versions "ST-N 300" AND "St-N 450", which were also standardised lifts for residential buildings with rotating shaft doors and wooden cabins without door terminations.
60. Winfried Nerdinger: "Materialästhetik und Rasterbauweise. Zum Charakter der Architektur der 50er Jahre" in: Werner Durth, Niels Gutschow: *Architektur und Städtebau der Fünfziger Jahre.* Bonn 1990, p. 39 (= series of publications of the German National Committee of Monument Preservation, volume 41).
61. *Grundlagen der Normungsarbeit des DIN.* Published by DIN Deutsches Institut für Normung e.V. Berlin/Vienna/Zürich 1995, p. 5.
62. Cf. DIN 15307 of 1952.
63. This is demonstrated by copies of the minutes of the meetings of the "Lifts" working party of 4th July 1952 in Königstein/Taunus and of 11th October 1957 in Frankfurt am Main.

damm erläutert der Autor, daß »die Ein- und Zwei-Zimmer-Wohnungen für Ein- bis Zwei-Personen-Haushalte [...] nicht von Scharoun projektiert [waren], sondern von der Firma vorgegeben, entworfen von Georg Jacobowitz«. (S. 70) Einen Quellenhinweis hierfür gibt er leider nicht.

45. Simmen/Drepper, wie Anm. 7, S. 90.
46. Laszlo Moholy-Nagy: *Von Material zu Architektur.* Faksimile der 1929 erschienenen Erstausgabe, Mainz/Berlin 1968, S. 222, Abb. 199.
47. Wolfgang Schäche: *Architektur und Städtebau in Berlin zwischen 1933 und 1945 – Planen und Bauen unter der Ägide der Stadtverwaltung.* Berlin 1992, S. 266-268.
48. H. Jaeger: *Bestimmungen über Einrichtung und Betrieb der Aufzüge.* Berlin 1930, S. 12.
49. Während die Polizeiverordnung vom 30. Mai 1913 noch eine Umwehrungshöhe von 1,80m vorschrieb, erhöhte sich diese ab 1926 auf eine Mindesthöhe von 2,50m. Die Höhe des Fahrkorbes muß mindestens 1,80 m betragen. Vgl. hierzu H. Jaeger, wie Anm. 48, S. 85 (Umwehrung), S. 86 (Türen), S. 104 (Fahrkorb).
50. Das Schild befindet sich im Archiv der Firma Gottschalk und Michaelis.
51. Vgl. hierzu Rundschreiben des Technischen Überwachungs-Vereins e.V. Berlin vom 17. Dezember 1942 im Archiv des TÜV.
52. *Die Welt* vom 25. Juni 1950.
53. H. Jaeger, wie Anm. 48, S. 16.
54. Simmen/Drepper, wie Anm. 7, S. 223–224.
55. *Zentralblatt der Bauverwaltung.* Nr. 20, 11. März 1908, S. 147.
56. Vgl. El Lissitzky: *Proun und Wolkenbügel – Schriften, Briefe, Dokumente.* hg. v. Sophie Lissitzky-Küppers und Jens Lissitzky, Dresden 1977, S. 82. El Lissitzky entwickelte das Wolkenbügel-Projekt in Zusammenarbeit mit Mart Stam (1899–1986) und Emil Roth.
57. Vgl. Bundesdeutsche Aufzugsverordnung vom 28. März 1972, Paragraph 28, im Bundesblatt; Verordnung über Aufzugsanlagen (Aufzugsverordnung), Paragraph 26, in: *TRA – Technische Regeln für Aufzüge.* Taschenbuchausgabe 1992, hg. v. Verband der Technischen-Überwachungs-Vereine e.V., Köln/Berlin 1992, S. 15.
58. *Berlin-Handbuch,* wie Anm. 19, S. 1389.
59. Otis entwickelte 1954 den »SWA« – Standard-Wohnhaus-Aufzug für vier Personen mit Schachtdrehtüren und Holzkabinen ohne Kabinenabschlüsse. Von Schindler stammen 1955 die Ausführungen »ST-N 300« und »St-N 450«, ebenfalls typisierte Aufzüge für den Wohnungsbau mit Schachtdrehtüren und Holzkabinen ohne Türabschlüsse.
60. Winfried Nerdinger: »Materialästhetik und Rasterbauweise. Zum Charakter der Architektur der 50er Jahre«, in: Werner Durth, Niels Gutschow: *Architektur und Städtebau der Fünfziger Jahre.* (= *Schriftenreihe des Deutschen National-*

komitees für Denkmalschutz, Band 41). Bonn 1990, S. 39
61. *Grundlagen der Normungsarbeit des DIN.* hg. v. DIN Deutsches Institut für Normung e.V., Berlin/Wien/Zürich 1995, S. 5.
62. Vgl. DIN 15307 von 1952.
63. Dies belegen Niederschriften der Sitzungsprotokolle des Arbeitsausschusses »Aufzüge« vom 4. Juli 1952 aus Königstein/Taunus und vom 11. Oktober 1957 aus Frankfurt am Main.
64. Vgl. hierzu *Aufzüge, Flurförderzeuge, Stetigförderer – Normen.* hg.v. DIN Deutsches Institut für Normung e.V., Berlin/Köln 1988, S. 279–284 (mit der aktualisierten Version vom Januar 1985).
65. *Aufzüge, Flurförderzeuge, Stetigförderer,* wie Anm. 54, S. 285–292 (mit der aktualisierten Version vom Dezember 1984).
66. Die Publikation von Jencks erschien 1977 in englischer und 1978 in deutscher Sprache. Einen Überblick über die verschiedenen Positionen zur Postmoderne bietet Wolfgang Welsch (Hg.): *Wege aus der Moderne – Schlüsseltexte der Postmoderne-Diskussion.* Berlin 1994.
67. Heinrich Klotz: *Moderne und Postmoderne – Architektur der Gegenwart 1960–1980.* Braunschweig/Wiesbaden (3. Aufl.) 1987, S. 136.
68. Vgl. Simmen/Drepper, wie Anm. 7, Abb. 1 – Frontispiz.
69. Helmut Jahn mit Patrick Krause und Rudolf Jeschenko: *Building Identity – Die Geschichte des grenzenlosen Erfolges.* Düsseldorf/Wien/New York/Moskau 1992, S. 200.
70. Falk Jaeger: »Familiengericht, Berlin 1989–1995«, in: *Centrum – Jahrbuch Architektur und Stadt 1995.* S. 156.
71. O.M. Ungers: »Maß, Zahl, Proportion«, in: Frank Barth (Hg.): *O.M. Ungers – Architekt.* Hamburg 1994, S. 10.
72. Vittorio Magnago Lampugnani: »Die Neue Einfachheit – Mutmaßungen über die Architektur der Jahrtausendwende«, in: Gert Kähler (Hg.): *Einfach – Eine deutsche Architekturdebatte, Ausgewählte Beiträge 1993–1995.* Braunschweig/Wiesbaden 1995, S. 24.
73. Falk Jaeger: *Zurück zu den Stilen.* Berlin 1991, S. 151.
74. Christina Haberlik, Gerwin Zohlen: *Die Baumeister des neuen Berlin – Porträts, Gebäude, Konzepte.* Berlin (2. Aufl.) 1998, S. 137.
75. Meinhard von Gerkan: *Von Gerkan, Marg und Partner – Architecture 1991–1995.* Basel/Boston/Berlin 1995, S. 6.
76. Haberlik/Zohlen, wie Anm. 74, S. 59.

64. Cf.: *Aufzüge, Flurförderzeuge, Stetigförderer – Normen.* Published by DIN Deutsches Institut für Normung e.V., Berlin/Cologne 1988, p. 279–284 (with the updated version of January 1985).
65. Ibid, p. 285-292 (with the updated version of December 1984).
66. Jencks' publication appeared in English in 1977 and in German in 1978. A survey of the various positions on Post-Modernism can be found in Wolfgang Welsch (ed.): *Wege aus der Moderne – Schlüsseltexte der Postmoderne-Diskussion.* Berlin 1994.
67. Heinrich Klotz: *Moderne und Postmoderne – Architektur der Gegenwart 1960–1980.* Braunschweig/Wiesbaden (3rd edition) 1987, p. 136.
68. Cf. Simmen/Drepper, op. cit., Fig. 1 – frontispiece.
69. Helmut Jahn with Patrick Krause and Rudolf Jeschenko: *Building Identity – Die Geschichte des grenzenlosen Erfolges.* Düsseldorf/Vienna/New York/Moscow 1992, p. 200.
70. Falk Jaeger: "Familiengericht, Berlin 1989–1995", in: *Centrum – Jahrbuch Architektur und Stadt.* 1995, p. 156.
71. O.M. Ungers: "Maß, Zahl, Proportion", in: Frank Barth (ed.): *O.M. Ungers – Architekt.* Hamburg 1994, p. 10.
72. Vittorio Magnago Lampugnani: "Die Neue Einfachheit – Mutmaßungen über die Architektur der Jahrtausendwende", in: Gert Kähler (ed.): *Einfach – Eine deutsche Architekturdebatte.* Selected contributions 1993–1995. Braunschweig/Wiesbaden 1995, p. 24.
73. Falk Jaeger: *Zurück zu den Stilen.* Berlin 1991, p. 151.
74. Christina Haberlik, Gerwin Zohlen: *Die Baumeister des neuen Berlin – Porträts, Gebäude, Konzepte.* Berlin (2nd edition) 1998, p. 137.
75. Meinhard von Gerkan: *Von Gerkan, Marg & Partner. Architektur 1991–1995.* Basel/Boston/Berlin 1995, p. 6.
76. Haberlik/Zohlen, op.cit., p. 59.

Selected Bibliography

Oliver Bachmann: *Aufzüge und Fahrtreppen. Technik, Planung und Design. (= Die Bibliothek der Technik, Band 66).* Landsberg/Lech 1992.

Berlin Und seine Bauten. Ed. by Architekten- und Ingenieur-Verein zu Berlin. Berlin 1964ff.

Berlin-Handbuch – Das Lexikon der Bundeshauptstadt. Ed. by Presse- und Informationsamt des Landes Berlin (Projektleitung: Ernst Luuk). Berlin 1993

Hugo Bethmann: *Der Aufzugbau.* Braunschweig 1913.

Carl Flohr Maschinenfabrik zum 50jährigen Bestehen des Unternehmens. Berlin 1900, reprint 1976.

Carl Flohr Berlin 1879–1904. Festschrift zur Feier des 25jährigen Geschäftsjubiläums am 2. Juli 1904. Berlin 1904.

Carl Flohr. 50 Jahre deutscher Aufzugsbau. Eine Festschrift zum 50jährigen Jubiläum der Carl Flohr A.G.. Berlin 1929.

Carl Ferdinand Franzen, Theodor Englert (Ed.): *Der Aufzugbau.* Braunschweig 1972.

Jean Gavois: *Going up.* Otis Elevator Company 1983.

Gottschalk & Michaelis. Reprint of an advertisement of 1913.

Peter Hirscher: *Aufzüge – Technik, Planung, Betrieb.* Thyssen-Aufzüge, München 1986.

Norbert Huse: *"Neues Bauen" 1918 bis 1933. Moderne Architektur in der Weimarer Republik.* München 1975.

Falk Jaeger: *Zurück zu den Stilen.* Berlin 1991.

H. Jaeger, U. Rühl, F. Wolter: *Bestimmungen über Einrichtung und Betrieb der Aufzüge.* Berlin (4th edition) 1930.

Vittorio Magnago Lampugnani, Lutz Hartwig (Ed.): *Vertikal – Aufzug, Fahrtreppe, Paternoster – Eine Kulturgeschichte vom Vertikal-Transport.* Berlin 1974.

Neue Architektur. Berlin 1990–2000. Ed. by the Förderverein Deutsches Architekturzentrum Berlin. Berlin 1997.

Otis Elevator Company. The first one hundred years 1853–1953. New York 1953.

Parallelen – Konsequenzen. Betrachtung einer fast 100-jährigen parallelen Entwicklung 1852–1951 und der 25 Jahre jungen Fusion 1951–1976. Flohr-Otis. Berlin 1976.

Wolfgang Schäche: *Architektur und Städtebau in Berlin zwischen 1933 und 1945. (= Die Bauwerke und Kunstdenkmäler von Berlin, Beiheft 17).* Berlin (2nd edition) 1992.

Schindler & Cie.. Aufzüge-Fabriken, Berlin gegründet 1906 – Luzern gegründet 1874. s.a.e.l.

Schindler. Das Phänomen der Gravitation. Ebikon e.l.

Jeannot Simmen, Uwe Drepper: *Der Fahrstuhl. Die der vertikalen Eroberung.* München 1984.

The Tyler Company. Elevator cars – Elevator entrances. Catalogue No. 56. Cleveland/Ohio 1927.

Martin Wörner, Doris Mollenschott, Karl-Heinz Hüter: *Architekturführer Berlin.* Berlin (5th edition) 1997.

Ausgewählte Literatur

Oliver Bachmann: *Aufzüge und Fahrtreppen. Technik, Planung und Design. (= Die Bibliothek der Technik, Band 66).* Landsberg/Lech 1992.

Berlin Und seine Bauten. Hg. v. Architekten- und Ingenieur-Verein zu Berlin. Berlin 1964ff.

Berlin-Handbuch – Das Lexikon der Bundeshauptstadt. Hg. v. Presse- und Informationsamt des Landes Berlin (Projektleitung: Ernst Luuk). Berlin 1993

Hugo Bethmann: *Der Aufzugbau.* Braunschweig 1913.

Carl Flohr Maschinenfabrik zum 50jährigen Bestehen des Unternehmens. Berlin 1900, Nachdruck 1976.

Carl Flohr Berlin 1879–1904. Festschrift zur Feier des 25jährigen Geschäftsjubiläums am 2. Juli 1904. Berlin 1904.

Carl Flohr. 50 Jahre deutscher Aufzugsbau. Eine Festschrift zum 50jährigen Jubiläum der Carl Flohr A.G.. Berlin 1929.

Carl Ferdinand Franzen, Theodor Englert (Hg.): *Der Aufzugbau.* Braunschweig 1972.

Jean Gavois: *Going up.* Otis Elevator Company 1983.

Gottschalk & Michaelis. Nachdruck einer Werbeschrift von 1913.

Peter Hirscher: *Aufzüge – Technik, Planung, Betrieb.* Thyssen-Aufzüge, München 1986.

Norbert Huse: *»Neues Bauen" 1918 bis 1933. Moderne Architektur in der Weimarer Republik.* München 1975.

Falk Jaeger: *Zurück zu den Stilen.* Berlin 1991.

H. Jaeger, U. Rühl, F. Wolter: *Bestimmungen über Einrichtung und Betrieb der Aufzüge.* Berlin (4. Aufl.) 1930.

Vittorio Magnago Lampugnani, Lutz Hartwig (Hg.): *Vertikal – Aufzug, Fahrtreppe, Paternoster – Eine Kulturgeschichte vom Vertikal-Transport.* Berlin 1974.

Neue Architektur. Berlin 1990–2000. Hg. v. Förderverein Deutsches Architekturzentrum Berlin. Berlin 1997.

Otis Elevator Company. The first one hundred years 1853–1953. New York 1953.

Parallelen – Konsequenzen. Betrachtung einer fast 100-jährigen parallelen Entwicklung 1852–1951 und der 25 Jahre jungen Fusion 1951–1976. Flohr-Otis. Berlin 1976.

Wolfgang Schäche: *Architektur und Städtebau in Berlin zwischen 1933 und 1945. (= Die Bauwerke und Kunstdenkmäler von Berlin, Beiheft 17).* Berlin (2. Aufl.) 1992.

Schindler & Cie.. Aufzüge-Fabriken, Berlin gegründet 1906 – Luzern gegründet 1874. O.O. o.J.

Schindler. Das Phänomen der Gravitation. Ebikon o.J.

Jeannot Simmen, Uwe Drepper: *Der Fahrstuhl. Die der vertikalen Eroberung.* München 1984.

The Tyler Company. Elevator cars – Elevator entrances. Catalogue No. 56. Cleveland/Ohio 1927.

Martin Wörner, Doris Mollenschott, Karl-Heinz Hüter: *Architekturführer Berlin.* Berlin (5. Aufl.) 1997.

Alfred Englert
Dipl.-Ing., von 1956 bis 1994 in der Aufzugsbranche tätig – davon 23 Jahre im Management. 25 Jahre Mitarbeit in nationalen und internationalen Normengremien. Darüber hinaus langjähriges Mitglied des Marketing-Club Berlin e.V.

Kerstin Englert
Kunsthistorikerin, von 1992 bis 1994 Wissenschaftliche Museumsassistentin i.F. bei den Staatlichen Museen zu Berlin Preußischer Kulturbesitz, seit 1994 Lehrbeauftragte an der Freien Universität Berlin. Verschiedene Publikationen zu Themen der Malerei und Architektur des 20. Jahrhunderts.

Alfred Englert
worked in the lift business from 1956 to 1994 – including 23 years in management. He served on national and international standardisation committees for 25 years. For many years he was a member of the Marketing-Club Berlin e.V.

Kerstin Englert
is an art historian. From 1992 to 1994 she was a scientific assistent at the *Staatliche Museen zu Berlin Preußischer Kulturbesitz* (Prussian Cultural Heritage Museum). She has lectured at the *Freie Universität Berlin*. Publications on various aspects of painting and architecture of the twentieth century.

Die Drucklegung wurde ermöglicht durch die freundliche Unterstützung der Schindler Aufzügefabrik GmbH.

jovis Verlagsbüro
Kurfürstenstraße 15/16
D–10785 Berlin

Frontispiz
Charlottenburg
1910 • Flohr
Wohnhaus *residential building*

Bildnachweis
AEG Archiv: S. 13
Gebr. Mann Verlag (Max Taut: *Bauten und Pläne*. Berlin 1996. Reprint der Erstausgabe): S. 58, Abb. 61
Otis GmbH: S. 12
Schindler Aufzügefabrik GmbH: S. 15, 60
Jeannot Simmen: S. 11, 61
Universitätsbibliothek Heidelberg: S. 10
Alle übrigen Abbildungen stammen von Alfred Englert.

Lektorat
Yamin von Rauch

Übersetzung ins Englische
Victor Dewsbury

Korrektur
Eva Cheung

Buchausstattung
Jürgen Freter, Berlin

Lithographie
Satzinform, Berlin

Druck und Bindung
Offizin Andersen Nexö Leipzig, Zwenkau

ISBN 3–931321–96–7